DEADMONTON

DEADMONTON

CRIME STORIES FROM CANADA'S MURDER CITY

BY PAMELA ROTH

University of Regina Press

Printed and bound in Canada at Friesens.

Cover design: Duncan Campbell, University of Regina Press
Text design: John Van der Woude, JVDW Designs
Copy editor: Meaghan Craven
Proofreader: Katie Sawatzky
Cover art: Material republished with the express permission of:
    Edmonton Journal, a division of Postmedia Network Inc.

Library and Archives Canada Cataloguing in Publication
Roth, Pamela, 1981-, author
    Deadmonton : crime stories from Canada's murder city / Pamela Roth.

Includes bibliographical references. Issued in print and electronic formats.
ISBN 978-0-88977-426-1 (paperback).—ISBN 978-0-88977-427-8 (pdf).—
ISBN 978-0-88977-428-5 (html)

1. Murder--Alberta--Edmonton--Case studies. I. Title.

HV6535.C33E4 2016   364.152'309712334   C2016-903858-0   C2016-903859-9

We acknowledge the support of the Canada Council for the Arts for
our publishing program. We acknowledge the financial support of the
Government of Canada. / Nous reconnaissons l'appui financier du
gouvernement du Canada. This publication was made possible through
Creative Saskatchewan's Creative Industries Production Grant Program.

This book is dedicated to the friends and families who've had loved ones taken away by murder. It is not meant to cause further pain or suffering, but instead to act as a collective memory of lives taken far too soon. It is also to serve as a reminder that many cases are still unsolved, and a single tip to police could change everything.

CONTENTS

ACKNOWLEDGEMENTS

I would like to thank several members and former members of the Edmonton Police Service and the RCMP for lending their time to talk about the investigations. I would also like to thank the victims' families for having the courage to speak about their loved ones, even though it is painful. I sincerely hope everyone will someday find closure.

INTRODUCTION

Five murders in one week. Two bodies found in a bullet-riddled SUV at a remote cemetery three months later. Then a desperate call for help to police from a man shot and stabbed several times, leaving another family torn apart by the sudden violent death of a loved one.

In 2011, Edmonton became the murder capital of Canada, when the tally of those killed reached forty-eight. There was no common pattern, single cause, or factor linking the slayings, so Edmonton police dubbed the high number of fatalities an anomaly. Still, it wasn't the first time the City of Champions had snagged the title no Canadian city wants to claim.

Alberta's capital also earned the same dubious distinction in 2005, when it recorded thirty-nine homicides, sparking a local newspaper to use the nickname for the city—Deadmonton—across its front page. Today, many of the killers still walk among the city's citizens, keeping their dark secrets to themselves.

Violence in Edmonton is nothing new. Even in 1938, the city had a higher per capita murder rate than Chicago. Dreams of striking it rich in the province's oil patch have lured all sorts of characters to the city from far and wide. Instead of finding wealth, some have found themselves locked up in the maximum-security prison northeast of

Edmonton that's also home to a women's institution, a psychiatric hospital, and the largest remand centre in Canada.

Housed in binders on a bookshelf at police headquarters are 190 unsolved homicides, the oldest dating back to February 11, 1938, when Fred Oliver was murdered at Dominion Motors. For twenty-nine of these cases, the police offer $40,000 rewards for information leading to an arrest. These rewards have been on the books for several years.

Many of the unsolved murders are gangster slayings; witnesses won't talk for fear of retaliation. Others are innocent lives snuffed out in the blink of an eye at the hands of strangers. These killings are the most chilling.

Murder cases that go unsolved are an emotional rollercoaster for victims' families. They experience a plethora of emotions as they struggle to cope with the horrendous pain of suddenly losing a loved one because of another human being. Some deal with the pain by pushing their emotions aside and carrying on with the daily rituals of life. Others become consumed by sadness, finding it difficult to function in society.

This book takes a look at some of Edmonton's most notorious solved and unsolved murders and provides a glimpse into the lives of the detectives working tirelessly to bring closure to families, whose constant sorrow is carried on the detectives' shoulders, making them hungry to put killers behind bars.

This book also profiles people that have been missing for decades, such as twenty-three-year-old Gail McCarthy, who vanished on her way to work at the Misericordia Hospital in November 1971. She was three months pregnant and had been married for five months. Her sisters have gone through tremendous pain and suffering not knowing what happened to Gail and will not rest until she is found.

These stories are not for the faint of heart. They are an eerie reminder of the horror humans are capable of inflicting upon each other. Told from the perspective of the victims' families, these accounts are shocking, gruesome, and filled with immense sadness and pain. Their common bond is the need for closure, no matter how much time has passed.

Thanks to advancements in DNA technology, some families have found closure long after they've lost hope for their loved ones' murders to be solved. Others continue to hope for some change, some new insight that will lead to some kind of conclusion—and they sometimes carry that hope with them to their graves.

When Nelson Plett and his younger brother Lyndon went to bed at night, their loving mother often tucked them in, sending them off to sleep. But on the evening of September 15, 1971, Nelson's mother wasn't there to say good night. Nor was she around the next day to see him off to school. Little did Nelson know that when he gave his mother a kiss at breakfast that morning, it would be the last time he would ever see her smiling face. At eight years old, his world was about to be turned upside down.

"We really didn't comprehend what was going on. It was a case of, *where's Mom? What's going on?*" said Nelson about the night his mother never came home. "There's no question there was something not quite right."

MaryAnn Plett was a deeply religious woman with strong ties to her husband, Jake. One of the city's first female real estate agents, the twenty-nine-year-old was working hard, trying to sell an acreage near Looma, approximately thirty kilometres southeast of Edmonton. A man who called himself James Cooper seemed to be her best chance at selling the property. Cooper claimed to be based out of Winnipeg, representing a large American mud-pump company in the oil industry. He needed a property with a clearing to store heavy equipment, and he wanted the view of the clearing to be blocked from the road for privacy. But Cooper didn't act like MaryAnn's usual clientele.

He pressed her for last-minute appointments at odd hours and was always late, even though he said he was in a big hurry. When he called her at her office at Graham Realty on Whyte Avenue, he wouldn't provide a return number or leave a message.

On the morning of September 15, 1971, Cooper arranged for MaryAnn to pick him up at the Bonnie Doon Shopping Centre at 11 a.m. By 5 p.m., when she didn't return to her office or home, her co-workers and husband thought something wasn't right. The police were called, and MaryAnn was reported missing.

"It was obvious that the complaint was legitimate. It wasn't just a missing person. There was more to it than just that," said eighty-year-old Al Gowler, who had been a detective with the Edmonton homicide unit for five years when MaryAnn disappeared. "As we got further into the investigation and started finding out different things, then it was pretty obvious that she had been taken against her will."

Nelson and his brother were used to an established routine. Normally, MaryAnn would come home around 5 p.m., and either she or Jake would make supper. When the realtors' office phoned the Plett residence looking for MaryAnn, Jake started to worry. He called places he thought she might be, but nobody had seen his five-foot-two, 120-pound wife anywhere.

A search of the Looma property that night also turned up nothing. The searchers had regrouped at the south-side Graham Realty office later that night when the unthinkable happened.

Jake was leaving the office around 11 p.m. when he saw a man slowly drive by in MaryAnn's green 1970 Pontiac

Laurentian. By the time he and MaryAnn's co-workers got to a vehicle to give chase, the car had already vanished.

Despite an exhaustive search of the city, it would be two days before a car attendant discovered the vehicle in the parking lot of Don Wheaton car sales, only a few blocks from MaryAnn's office.

There was damage to the front fender and a small gouge in a rear tire. Grass stalks were stuck in the front bumper and a two-foot-long tree branch was wedged in the under-carriage, indicating the car had been driven off-road. The contents of the glove compartment were missing, along with MaryAnn's purse and notebook. Blood matching her type was found on the rug in the trunk and along the trunk's latch. A wig she wore sometimes was also found inside the trunk. Police lifted a fingerprint from the driv-er's door, but it was unsuitable for comparison using the techniques of the day. The only other thing left behind was a pack of DuMaurier cigarettes and a pair of slip-over sunglasses. At this point, Al had little hope MaryAnn was still alive.

"We were very disappointed that the car hadn't been found earlier," he said. "Whether it would have done any good, I don't know. With the wig and some clothing and the blood and the trunk, it was quite obvious she was dead. There was nothing that belonged to this guy that you could get DNA material off for a sample. He was very, very careful. He went to great lengths to make sure that nobody else saw him except her. He never gave her a phone num-ber; he never gave her an address. It was always a 'don't call me, I'll call you' type of thing.

"She remarked to somebody that he was always late, and yet here was a guy who said he was in a big hurry and he only had a short period of time to look at this," Al went on. "So it doesn't make sense that he was going to be late for an appointment. That tells me that he was sitting back, watching her and making sure that she was alone. He's a predator. He set up things the way he wanted."

Not long after MaryAnn's disappearance, another female real estate agent received a call from a man with a deep gravelly voice who identified himself as Dave Cooper. He also claimed to be from the east and wanted to see an acreage property out of town, but the realtor was too busy to schedule the viewing.

As news spread about MaryAnn's mysterious disappearance, hundreds of tips about her whereabouts began pouring in to police, but most of them were outrageous. One of the tipsters was a man who claimed to know where MaryAnn was because he had held a ring on a piece of string over a map and it went to a certain area. Other psychics had similar far-fetched ideas about where she might be. Another search of the Looma area brought out nearly two hundred real estate agents, church members, relatives, and people with no connection to the Plett family, but once again there was no sign of MaryAnn.

Although he was just a child, Nelson felt the stress oozing from his father and relatives. For the first couple of days, he didn't comprehend what was going on, but he felt hurt his mother hadn't come home. Nelson describes those days as a blur, with a lot of people coming and going.

Since MaryAnn's keys and personal items were missing, safety precautions were taken when Nelson and Lyndon went to school. Then the nightmares began, and the full gravity of the situation hit Nelson like a ton of bricks.

"My dad did his best to shelter us from certain details, but realistically, I was hip-deep in it because how do you not be? Your mom's not around, you are surrounded by strangers, you have to be picked up from school. None of that stuff was normal," he said.

Seven months passed before MaryAnn's remains were found in a wooded area one hundred kilometres northwest of Edmonton. In April 1972, two employees of the Pinto Creek Sawmill were digging a trench when they found the tattered remains of women's clothing scattered along Goose Lake Road. Those clothes were taken to the police. A further search of the area by authorities found a watch given to MaryAnn by her mother, along with the top portion of a human skull and part of a femur. The remains were identified as being MaryAnn's through dental records, but the cause of death remains a mystery. The contents of the glove compartment, MaryAnn's purse, and her notebook have never been recovered.

Nelson remembers the moment his mother's remains were found like it was yesterday. It was the missing piece of the puzzle everyone had been waiting for.

"Dad called us in the house. I remember seeing my grandmother coming to the house. I remember when they told us, just completely breaking down," said Nelson. "It's the finality of it. Deep down, I kind of suspected there was no chance that Mom was coming back, but when they finally told us and said, okay, this is literally what had happened, they found Mom's body, then I suddenly went, okay."

Working with the RCMP, Al spent months following up on various leads. His RCMP counterparts did everything imaginable to solve the case, but to this day the killer has yet to be found.

Given the remote location of the remains, Al believes the killer was familiar with Edmonton and the surrounding area and that it was possible he was a hunter or an outdoorsman.

The case puzzles Al to this day. Because so many questions remain unanswered, he doubts it will ever be solved.

"The simplest case can be the most baffling until it's solved. It's one of those things that you still think about. There is absolutely nothing to tie anybody in with this thing," said Al, noting the file has been turned over to the RCMP. "It's not a case that would be sitting on somebody's desk, but it wouldn't be closed, either. Whenever anything came up, the file would be brought back to light, and if there were something legitimate to follow up then it would be. Most cold cases, they are never closed. They are kept open and available."

Nelson Plett holds a picture of his mother, MaryAnn Plett, who went missing in the Looma area, thirty kilometres southeast of Edmonton, on September 15, 1971. (Photo by Darren Makowichuk / Courtesy of Sun Media)

Jake went on with life as best he could, eventually remarrying, but he continued to work tirelessly on solving MaryAnn's murder. He penned a book about the case, titled *Valley of Shadows*, but no new significant information emerged as a result of its publication. Jake's quest to find the killer ended in 1978 when he and his wife, along with forty others, died in a plane crash in Cranbrook, B.C. Nelson misses his father every day. Some days are harder than others.

Nelson still speaks with the RCMP from time to time. In 2010 detectives took some blood samples from him and his brother, which, paired with new technology, might help solve the case. The nightmares have now tapered off, and Nelson has a family of his own in Calgary. Although it's been forty-one years since his mother's death, he still wants to see the killer put behind bars. The thought of having closure someday never goes away.

"My dad always said that, if and when this guy was ever caught, he would go and tell him that he forgave him. My brother and I both said, as difficult as it might be, if it was ever solved, we would try and honour dad's wishes," said Nelson, noting the tragedy brought his extended family closer together.

"We were very fortunate we were a very close family, and I was always surrounded by that family. You can't help but be scarred by what I've been through. You get to the point where you kind of go, *there's a reason for this*. You don't always understand the reason, and you hope some day you will, but you may not. It makes you who you are. You learn to value family and those that are close to you very, very deeply."

KAREN EWANCIW

April 23, 1975, was a day that filled Shelley Campbell with so much fear that she's spent a lifetime hiding.

Shelley was only ten years old when she and her eleven-year-old friend, Karen Ewanciw, decided that instead of delivering their flyers after school, they would dump them in the river valley that bordered their quiet Forest Heights neighbourhood in southeast Edmonton. The densely wooded ravine wasn't a place the two inseparable best friends would usually go to play, but on this particular day they agreed it was where they would head after school and pretend to be partners in crime.

Shelley noticed some unusual things the moment the pair entered the ravine from the top of the hill by McNally High School. They came across a pornography magazine beside the footpath, then cotton balls that appeared to have blood on them. The two friends continued walking deeper into the woods and found a massive spruce tree with a beautiful upside down cross sitting at its base. Shelley immediately got a creepy feeling and warned Karen to leave the cross alone, but her friend was drawn toward it like a kid in a candy store.

"I told her not to touch it, begging her, almost to the point where I was in tears," said Shelley. "I just knew by the feeling that it was giving me that it was pure evil and

[I thought], don't touch this cross. She didn't listen to me. She picked it up and wanted to keep it."

Karen eventually put the cross back down and left it behind as the kids continued their adventure through the ravine. They came to a hill and decided to slide down. Karen went first, and she kept all her flyers in a bundle as she slid to the bottom. Shelley, however, tipped over, spilling her flyers all over the ground. While Shelley picked up her flyers, Karen walked off in a trance, despite her friend's repeated calls to wait.

"I cried out to her. Here we were being partners in crime, and all of a sudden she's walking away from me?" said Shelley. "I called to her a few times, and she wouldn't even turn around. She didn't acknowledge me; she didn't do anything. It was really bizarre."

Shelley last saw Karen walking toward the main path that runs through the ravine. Then she disappeared. A baffled Shelley quickly gathered her flyers and went looking for her friend, but she had no luck. With no trace of Karen anywhere, Shelley began to feel scared.

"By this time my hair was basically standing up and something was telling me this was really not good," she said. "How does your best friend disappear? Why would she walk away from me?"

It was eerily quiet. Not even the birds were chirping in the maze of spruce and poplar trees along the river. Suddenly, a rush of wind sent a frightened Shelley flying out of the ravine. At the top of the hill sitting on a bench was a classmate. Shelley asked if he had seen Karen, but he said no. Still in shock, she headed home, hoping to hear from her friend soon, but she never did.

Shelley went to school the next day, pretending everything was normal. She expected to see Karen in class, but she never came to school. Police contacted Shelley's mother and pulled the young girl out of class. She was given the grim news that her best friend had been found, but not alive. The news of Karen's death didn't hit Shelley until she was watching the news that evening in her family's living room by herself.

"I still remember this—just watching [on the news] her being carried out on a stretcher," said Shelley, struggling to keep back tears. "That's when it was real to me. I was completely in shock."

Less than twenty-four hours after the two friends had wandered into the ravine, a jogger running through the area found Karen's five-foot-two, 85-pound body about fifteen metres from a well-used footpath. She was lying on her face in a small wooded area. Her clothing had been violently stripped from her body and hung on low-lying branches, indicating the assailant had chased her down

Former Edmonton Police Detective Ron Johnson holds a picture of eleven-year-old murder victim Karen Ewanciw near the location where she was found in 1975. (Photo by Perry Mah / Courtesy of Sun Media)

and dragged her into the shelter of the trees before sexually assaulting her.

An autopsy later confirmed Karen had suffered a massive skull fracture during the savage attack. At the scene, investigators discovered a large piece of knotted wood and several pieces of birch nearby with what appeared to be Karen's hair embedded in them. Police believe the attacker used a thick tree branch to deliver the massive blow to the young girl's head. The blow was so fierce that an imprint of Karen's face was left in the soft earth where she came to a final rest.

Due to her extensive injuries, dental records were required to accurately confirm Karen's identity. A medical examination revealed Karen had severe fingernail depressions on her face and bruising on her neck, shoulders, and lower extremities.

The brutal murder of such a young girl rocked the community, as details of the grisly crime spread. Detective Ron Johnson remembers seeing photos of Karen's body during his recruit training to become a police officer in 1981. The photos were so horrific, he was left wondering if he had made the right career move.

Years later, Ron began working on the case. In 2005 he was involved in a Crime Stoppers re-enactment where Karen was found. It was an experience that wasn't easy, even for veteran detectives.

"Watching the look on his [one of the original investigators] face when he was walking down the path to show us where everything was, his eyes were glassed over. You could tell, even after all this time, it still had an effect on him," said Ron. "It was absolutely horrible—just the random brutality of it. It shook the whole city."

The search for the person responsible for Karen's death has hit one wall after another. Despite suspect interviews, witness statements, tips, and advancements in forensic evidence review developed across North America, the killer has yet to be found and the case has gone cold. However, several pieces of evidence and witness testimony have led detectives to a shortlist of what are deemed to be people of interest. Investigators believe the assailant lived in or near the Forest Heights and McNally area in the 1970s, but the missing link that will put the case to rest will likely come from the public.

Ron helped track down a suspect one of the initial investigators had in mind, but the man had Alzheimer's and there was nothing to indicate he was involved with Karen's murder.

"He just happened to live in the neighbourhood and was one of the last people to see Karen and her friend before she was murdered," said Ron. "He was walking around when the body was found. We talked to members of his family, and this guy had never done anything violent or weird. There was nothing to tie him in."

The young, mischievous Karen, who had developed physically at a young age, was one of four daughters her father, Walter Ewanciw, was trying to raise on his own. Despite the loss of his child, Walter had to stay strong for his family, even though he knew his daughters were struggling to cope with the senseless death of their sister. He doesn't believe the attack was random and claims to know who killed Karen. The problem, he said, is that the man is no longer alive. Walter regrets not taking care of the killer himself while he had the chance.

Although thirty-seven years have passed, eighty-two-year-old Walter still has a hard time talking about his daughter's unsolved murder. From the get-go, he wasn't hopeful the case would be solved.

"I didn't have faith in the justice system. I just thought that was it, wash it off. The way those police at the time were working, it wouldn't have been solved," said Walter. "You can't bring her back, and there were three other ones to look after yet. You just had to wash that away, and that was it."

Life for Walter didn't get any easier. Since Karen's death, he's had to bury two of his other daughters who died before reaching fifty due to health problems.

And life for Shelley didn't get much better, either. Following Karen's death, she was taken in for questioning by police, beginning a personal hell that robbed her of a childhood. Instead of being interviewed, Shelley claims she was interrogated and made to feel like it was her responsibility to solve the crime, even though she was a ten-year-old child.

"She [a police officer] was drilling it into my head that I knew who killed my friend. She wasn't being comforting. Nobody was consoling me. I was by myself at ten years old to deal with this stuff," said Shelley. "The detectives put the fear of God in me not to talk about this. I've tried to talk to the detectives about certain things, and there are only certain things that they want to listen to. I've basically given them my life to help solve this case."

Shelley has no doubt the killer saw her in the ravine that day, playing with her friend, but she has no idea who it could be. She believes it was somebody Karen knew, given the way Karen walked away from Shelley's calls to wait. Walter, however, believes Shelley saw the killer, even though she remembered nothing of him when placed under hypnosis to see if any suppressed memories would emerge.

Karen's death turned Shelley's world upside down. Due to safety concerns, she wasn't allowed to go to school or attend Karen's funeral. The lack of contact with the Ewanciw family was the icing on the cake of her emotional turmoil.

"We were ripped apart. It would have been wonderful to just cry like sisters. All my parents did was send her family flowers," said Shelley, who now has three children of her own. When her oldest daughter turned ten, her paranoia intensified.

"Seeing my oldest daughter as a ten-year-old child and looking at her, I saw myself. That's when my brain had to reconnect with my body."

Struggling to cope with the tragedy, Shelley turned to drugs, but even that couldn't numb the pain. By the time the twenty-fifth anniversary of Karen's death rolled around in 2000, Shelley felt like a walking zombie and contemplated taking her life during a visit to Karen's unmarked grave. The only thing that stopped her was not wanting to hurt her own family. Shelley also made a visit to the scene of the crime for the first time, only to discover it opened wounds that have never healed. She's spent a lifetime trying to disassociate herself from Karen's death, spending many days living in fear, wondering if the killer is hunting for her. Dealing with survivor's guilt has been a constant struggle.

"I'm still running after thirty-seven years. I am still this ten-year-old girl, but in a grown woman's body. It doesn't go away. We just have to learn to deal with it. Even if they do find who killed Karen, that's not going to really change anything," said Shelley. "I should have never made it out of that ravine. I know whoever killed her was after me, and something protected me. It would have been a lot easier to have died with Karen."

Twelve years ago, Shelley finally found the right support network to help her deal with her ongoing grief. She also attended meetings with a victims-of-homicide support group that provided comfort, but even then she continued to suck back her tears. Stuffing her emotions inside is a practice Shelley has become used to, despite the additional stress it's created for her tiny body, which is now plagued by illness. Her family has been there to support her, but talking to them about her pain is difficult.

After thirty-seven years, Shelley decided to break her silence and go public with her story. It's something she felt she had to do if she wanted to make it to her fiftieth birthday and find peace.

"I am really looking forward to my fiftieth birthday. I am excited to find out what is in store for me. I can't continue living my life being a victim." Still, she says, "It's very, very sad. That's the whole thing about this—the sadness."

HUB MALL TRIPLE MURDER

Xavier Rejano has declared himself the man of the house. It wasn't supposed to be that way. He's only eight years old.

When his father, Eddie Rejano, was gunned down in a robbery massacre at the University of Alberta in June 2012, Xavier promised he was going to be the man of the house for his mom and five-year-old brother, Xylar. Not a day goes by when Eddie, thirty-nine at the time of his death, isn't in his family's hearts and minds.

"Xavier just talks about Daddy most of the time, and I encourage them to talk about him every day," said Eddie's wife, Cleo Badon, adding it feels like the shooting happened yesterday. Some days are harder than others when it comes to coping with the loss.

"I find myself awash in grief so fresh it threatens to drown me, but the boys are the ones that keep me going, and I can only hope that they will become the people we want them to be when they're older."

June 15 is a day Cleo will never forget. Neither will the families of Eddie's colleagues, Michelle Shegelski, twenty-six, Brian Ilesic, thirty-five, and Corporal Matthew Schuman, twenty-six.

Shortly after midnight, the four armoured car guards were exchanging funds at a bank machine inside the

University of Alberta's HUB Mall—a shopping centre and residence on the campus. They were also in the company of another employee, twenty-one-year-old Travis Baumgartner.

The five were on a routine circuit, replenishing money in ATMs throughout the city. Four of them entered a secure vestibule providing access to two machines at HUB Mall when Baumgartner removed his .38-calibre handgun from its holster. He shot Matthew once in the head, then moved on to Michelle, shooting her once in the head and then Brian twice. Michelle and Brian were killed instantly, but Matthew was still somehow alive.

Baumgartner left his victims locked inside the vestibule and reloaded his gun in the mall stairwell before going back outside. He approached the armoured car where Eddie was waiting for his colleagues and shot him underneath his right eye, then twice in the back of the head before speeding away in the armoured vehicle.

While Baumgartner was fleeing, several police officers responded to the bloody scene, using a pickaxe and bolt cutters to get into the locked vestibule from where they could hear Matthew's anguished cries for help. Matthew was rushed to hospital where he underwent surgery to remove the bullet lodged in his head; he was then placed into a medically induced coma.

In the moments leading up to the bloodshed, Ian Breitzke was about to close his window and head to bed when he heard what sounded like a gunshot outside the student residence where he was living. At first, the accounting student, who was in the final year of his degree, dismissed it as being something else, since there was always something going on in the area. Nothing seemed out of the ordinary when he looked outside his window. A few seconds later, however, Ian heard another three to five gunshots, followed by somebody screaming in pain.

"I thought, there's clearly somebody getting shot outside the building. I'm definitely going to lock the door and probably not going anywhere right now," said Ian, who watched the chaos unfold below his window.

Responding to the mayhem before the police arrived, University Safewalk volunteers called to Matthew from outside the locked bank machine vestibule where he was trapped. Minutes later, emergency crews arrived and began pulling out three lifeless bodies. Ian couldn't believe what he was witnessing. Questions about who did this and why began swirling through his head.

"It's definitely not something I want to see again, of course. I know that it's kind of an isolated event," said Ian, adding the incident was over in less than a minute. "It definitely has an impact on you."

News of the shooting spread quickly on social media throughout the university. Some students turned to Twitter to ask what was going on. Others reported hearing sirens, loud banging noises, and being in "lockdown" in their buildings at around 12:30 a.m. It wasn't until 1:15 a.m. that all students were notified about the horrific attack over HUB Mall's intercom system.

"It's pretty shocking. You never think something like that could happen," said one student, adding the school was busy, with final exams and a conference taking place.

Police immediately taped off the entire area surrounding HUB Mall and cleared the inside, setting up a command post. A black tarp was set up underneath the mall's ped-way where Eddie was shot dead. Michelle and Brian were removed from the bank machine vestibule.

Some of the officers responding to the bloody scene were impacted by what they saw. One of them told a newspaper photographer it was "the worst thing I've ever seen."

"Our investigators have described the scene as one of unimaginable carnage," said Police Chief Rod Knecht. "The tragic nature of the crime scene has been a challenge for some of our staff, and we look to provide them with support and counseling in the weeks to come."

Police later surrounded an armoured car outside the *Edmonton Sun* press plant at 9300 47th Street. Surveillance footage from the press plant, adjacent to the G4S Security parking lot, showed the driver getting out of the armoured car before 1 a.m. He then got into a waiting truck and sped away.

Ten hours later, Rod Knecht told the nation the hunt was on for Baumgartner. Officers closed in on the Sherwood Park home where he had been living with his parents, but Baumgartner was nowhere to be found. Canada-wide warrants were issued for his arrest on charges of three counts of first-degree murder and one count of attempted murder. Baumgartner's mother pleaded for him to come home.

"I'm sorry we had an argument [Thursday] night...but I want you to come home and do the right thing," said Sandy Baumgartner in a statement read by Edmonton police.

"Trav, as your mother, I ask that you come forward and take responsibility for your actions."

Police were asking the public to be on the lookout for a dark-blue Ford F-150 pickup truck with plates that might have been swapped. They also believed Baumgartner was armed and dangerous, and they advised anyone who encountered him to use extreme caution.

When Baumgartner rolled up to the United States border thirty-six hours later, agents already knew who he was. The murder suspect had his face plastered all over the news, along with his vehicle, and he was now trying to cross into the U.S. at the Lynden, Washington, border, south of Abbotsford, B.C. The dark-blue Ford still had his mother's licence plate attached to the vehicle. The plate was scanned on its way to the booth, where officers were waiting to make an arrest.

"We start making commands.... We don't ask, 'How's your day?'" said a U.S. Customs and Border Protection officer. "By the time a vehicle and its occupants arrive at the point of entry, we have a pretty good idea who's inside."

No weapons were found inside the truck, but Baumgartner did have a backpack containing more than $300,000 cash. The capture came just hours after police issued another plea for friends who might have had contact with Baumgartner to come forward.

Henrietta Shegelski clearly remembers the way her son Victor's voice sounded on the message he left on her phone that day in June. She knew something terrible had happened just by his tone.

"It [his tone] was totally devastated. There was so much emotion pent up that it had to come out," she said from her home in Lac du Bonnet, Manitoba. "When I did call him back, I said, 'What's wrong?' and the tears just flooded out."

The first time Henrietta met Michelle she knew she was special, the kind of woman every mother wants her son to marry. The pair had exchanged vows just seven weeks earlier, in April. They had met when Victor, a former soldier who completed two tours in Afghanistan with the Canadian Forces, started working at G4S three years prior. Michelle's death devastated Victor, but he's since dived into his university studies, working on his thesis in Honduras.

"It's helped him a great deal to cope with things. He's still got a long way to go before he's going to be back to the old Victor. She was a very special person in his life," said Henrietta. "It still hurts, but I can remember the happy times and end up with a smile rather than tears most of the time."

Brian left behind his thirteen-year-old daughter, Kiannah, for whom friends said he had unflinching devotion. A trust fund for her education has been set up in her name.

For Matthew's future father-in-law, Don McCarroll, everything about that tragic day is a blur. He received an emotional phone call from his daughter at around 2:30 a.m. and was on the plane to Edmonton from Toronto six hours later, bracing himself for the worst. Before Don knew it, he was at the hospital, the family thrown into turmoil, not knowing if Matthew would survive.

"We are pleased to no end that Matt has done as well as he has. It's just amazing. You look at him and think nothing happened," said Don, calling Matthew's recovery a miracle. "It's a matter of trying to understand the new reality. It's still a journey. It's not finished."

Matthew was a full-time air-force firefighter with the Canadian Forces in Edmonton and worked part-time with the security company. He spent four months in the hospital before returning home to his son, Landen. Another four months were spent attending rehab almost daily, wearing a helmet while his injury healed. Doctors told Matthew's mother that he might never walk or read again, but the more he walked, the more he wanted to get up and go. In an interview with CBC News in March 2013, Matthew told his story for the first time.

"What I had thought was that they were unconscious with me like I was. I didn't know I was shot in the head.

I didn't know anything. I could smell the blood," said Matthew about the shooting.

"The last thing I can remember hearing—which I found out later—it was the police ramming the door in. I thought I was being shot again, so that's why I was screaming even harder. Then all of a sudden it was just really peaceful."

The deaths of the three guards left deep wounds on their grieving families and friends, and fellow employees with G4S Cash Solutions had a tough time coping as well. Some employees suddenly had issues with trust. Management was in constant contact with staff.

"People who had been working for us for years and years were a little bit hesitant to work with more junior employees they didn't know as well," said company spokesperson Katie McLeod. "It was actually a major concern for us when it first happened, but it honestly didn't last very long."

In the months leading up to the murders, Baumgartner displayed several warning signs that something was up. He jokingly texted a friend, saying he was going to rob G4S. A number of posts were also placed on his Facebook page, boasting that he'd been given a gun following training and he was a "god" as a result of a perfect shooting test. Even more chilling was a post in which he wondered if he would make the 6 p.m. news if he started popping people off. Along with that post was a picture of him wearing a vest, a balaclava, and sunglasses.

In an online dating profile, Baumgartner described himself as a great guy, the kind that doesn't come along very often. He posted a shirtless photo of himself posing in front of the mirror and a picture of the truck police later would be looking for. Baumgartner further described himself as a person who lived to work out and loved talking, and he said he had been told he looked like a "ten." His ambition was to better the world, and he noted his profession as an armoured guard.

"I intend to become a CEO of a major corporation and use my power to help everyone I can," said Baumgartner in his profile. "I'm easy to get to know and I'm very laid back."

A former schoolmate described Baumgartner as a quiet kid who got bullied a lot.

"He was into paintball and stuff like that...he never seemed angry, just quiet," said the schoolmate. "Happy, good-spirited guy, too."

With their only child now in custody, an emotional Sandy Baumgartner and her husband told CTV News they were sorry for the pain the families of the four victims were suffering. The crime committed by their son left the

Left: Michelle Shegelski. (Photo courtesy of Sun Media); Right: Brian Ilesic with his daughter, Kiannah. (Photo courtesy of Sun Media)

couple heartbroken, devastated, and struggling to under-stand why it happened. Only a week before the shootings, Baumgartner had e-mailed his mother an application for the city police to print off and bring home.

"There [are] not even words to say how sorry we are for what has happened to these victims and the families that are involved," said Sandy through tears. "If we could take it back, if there was anything that could be done."

On the night before the murders, Baumgartner had fought with his mother over rent money he owed and told her not to worry, stating he wasn't coming back home, but she would get her money. Sandy went to bed after her son went to work his night shift. She heard about the shooting when she woke up the next day and noticed her son wasn't home, even though his work boots were at the front door. A large bundle of cash was on the kitchen table—an esti-mated $64,000. Sandy had no idea where her son could be.

In September 2013, a hulking and pale-faced Baumgartner pleaded guilty to one count of first-degree murder, two counts of second-degree murder, and one count of attempted murder. Both the Crown and defence put forward a joint submission for a life sentence with no eligibility of parole for forty years—the harshest sentence imposed in Canada since the country's last executions in 1962. This meant the twenty-two-year-old would not be eli-gible for parole until the age of sixty-one.

Chief Crown Prosecutor Steven Bilodeau called Baumgartner's actions "cowardly" and "heinous," a treacherous betrayal of his co-workers' trust that sent shockwaves across the world. Defence lawyer Peter Royal said it was "as terrible a multiple crime as they come," and he informed the packed room that Baumgartner did not want to address the court. There would be no answers from the accused that day for his senseless and obscenely cruel crime.

The court proceedings did, however, reveal more details about Baumgartner's path after he pulled the trigger. The cold-blooded killer went back to the G4S worksite where he removed three packages of cash, estimated to be $360,000, got into his pickup truck, and drove away. He dropped some of the cash off at the homes of two friends before heading to his mother's for a change of clothes and to leave that bundle of cash on her kitchen table.

Baumgartner then drove west, stopping in Banff to discard his gun and vest in a river. At the border, where he was arrested, Baumgartner told officers he didn't remember anything, and he claimed an armed man told him to drive the backpack to Seattle and deliver it to him or his family would be killed.

The following day, when questioned by Edmonton police, Baumgartner told officers his name was David Webb—the name of fictional assassin Jason Bourne from

Eddie Rejano with his wife, Cleo Baden. (Photo courtesy of Cleo Baden)

the novels and movies. Baumgartner also said he had been told he had killed three people, but that he couldn't recall anything.

He later admitted to the killings, telling investigators he had been "mad at the world." In a blind rage he aimed for the victims' heads when he pulled the trigger.

Plenty of tears were shed as the highly emotional victim impact statements were read in court following Baumgartner's guilty pleas.

Matthew lost a large portion of his brain and suffers from seizures due to his injury. He's also lost vision in the right half of both eyes and lives with constant pain.

"People say I am one of the lucky ones. I can promise you, most days it doesn't feel like that. I don't feel lucky that I lived and they all died," wrote Matthew, who wasn't present during the court proceedings. But for Baumgartner, he had a message, "I hope you have a long life, because I want you to have the time to think about what you did and all the hurt and pain you caused and continue to cause."

Brian's parents, Mike and Dianne, stood together crying as Dianne read their statement, telling Baumgartner he had left them "nothing but memories and sorrow and empty hearts."

Eddie's wife Cleo stated she never thought she'd become a widow at the age of thirty-two.

During the sentencing hearing, Court of Queen's Bench Justice John Rooke used the words "horrendous," "outrageous," "senseless," and "cowardly" to describe Baumgartner's crimes.

"Those were assassinations and executions callously carried out by a cold-blooded killer with no regard for human life, all for the simple motive of robbery," said Justice Rooke. Baumgartner sat slumped in the prisoner's box, seemingly disinterested, with his arms folded across his chest and his eyes often closed during the three-hour hearing.

Families of the victims were relieved by the harsh sentence, calling it a victory. But in reality, it still seems like a nightmare.

"Now I get to contribute my tax money to keep a killer alive, so that's definitely disappointing," said Michelle's widower, Victor. "I think he should just be taken out behind the shed and put down. Personally, that's my opinion."

RED LIGHT LOUNGE MASSACRE

As shocking as the execution-style deaths were of three armoured-car guards conducting their duties at the University of Alberta in June 2012, it wasn't the first time the city of Edmonton had experienced a triple murder.

In October 2006, Jacey Pinnock gave his mother a big hug and flashed a few of his dance moves before heading out for a night on the town. On this particular Saturday, club goers would have an extra hour to party as the clocks moved back one hour for daylight savings.

Dave Persaud was also eager for a night on the town after working nearly a month straight. He arrived at the Red Light Lounge around 12:30 a.m. with two friends. The place was quiet, with only a dozen people inside.

A half hour later, the party picked up when about a hundred people flowed through the front door, including Jacey and Thomas Tip Orak. Each arrived with his own group of friends. Dwayne Nelson was among Jacey's crew.

By 2 a.m. the dance floor was hopping, and about 150 people were now packed inside the downtown club. In a friendly competition, one of Dave's friends began a dance-off that lasted until a fight broke out somewhere on the dance floor among about ten men. Dave went over to try and break it up, but he was punched in the process.

Incensed, and caught up in the moment, he rushed across the dance floor and grabbed a beer bottle, breaking it over someone's head.

A larger brawl ignited but came to an end when bouncers threw some of the troublemakers out of the club. Suffering from a cut, Dave decided to go to the hospital. Jacey told his friends he was going home. Thomas planned to do the same, but the exit to the front door was slowed by the mass of people trying to leave after the violence.

Dwayne was one of the men involved in the brawl. The twenty-two-year-old supposedly heard that some of his opponents were going to get weapons, so he went outside and grabbed a gun he had stashed in a van.

When he returned, Dwayne held the 9mm Glock pistol in his pocket, and as tempers continued to flare, Dwayne pulled out the gun and started firing into the crowd, hitting his own friend, Jacey, in the process. The gunfire turned the mass exodus into mass panic as frightened patrons tried to duck for cover near walls and under pool tables. Thomas, an eighteen-year-old Sudanese refugee, was caught in the crossfire as he was leaving the bar.

"All I see is [a man] start popping the gun five, six times," said Thomas's best friend Bolis Wol. "I look and my friend was down. I just went to him. I was shocked. I went to see if he was breathing. It was too late."

Thomas was hit once in the head. Jacey was hit in the chest near his armpit, leading his mother and friends to believe he was trying to grab the gun away from Dwayne.

One of Dave's friends splashed water on Jacey's and Thomas's faces, desperately trying to revive them, but he could tell they were already dead. Both friends then noticed Dave breathing slowly, not talking, just looking at them. Inside the dark club, they noticed a toonie-size bloodstain near his left shoulder, and they splashed water on his face, too. They failed to realize he had been shot twice in the chest. The twenty-one-year-old from Toronto died in the ambulance on the way to the hospital.

When police arrived at the chaotic scene, Thomas and Jacey were indeed already dead, and three others, including a bouncer, were wounded. The three men who had been fatally shot had never met before they died. It was Edmonton's worst homicide in nearly three decades.

Police locked down the area around the club, blocking vehicles and pedestrian traffic in front of the scene. More than twenty suspects were interviewed, but no one was immediately taken into custody.

A few hours later, Veronica Pinnock's phone was ringing off the hook with news that her twenty-seven-year-old son Jacey was one of three male victims of a shooting

A body is removed from the Red Light Lounge after multiple shots rang out in the early morning hours of October 29, 2006. (Photo courtesy of Sun Media)

spree at a downtown club that catered mainly to patrons of African and Caribbean descent.

"They said there was a fight, and he was stopping it and he got shot," said Veronica, who described her son as a happy person, the father of a ten-month-old boy. "We're positive that it's him. He's not here. He didn't come home."

Born in Toronto, Jacey moved with his family to Edmonton in 1980. He started getting into trouble twenty years later for weapons offenses and drug trafficking. But the recent arrival of his child seemed to have turned the once-troubled man around. He had enrolled in an online real estate course and almost never went anywhere without his son.

"He just changed for the best," said his mother "He want[ed] to have something his baby [could] live for. Now he's gone."

A few days after the shocking violence, police arrested Dwayne and charged him with three counts of second-degree murder, along with two counts of aggravated assault and one count of assault causing bodily harm. When the arrest was made, Thomas's grieving family gathered around their television to catch a glimpse of the man accused of killing their loved one.

"We just want to see what he looks like...to see what kind of a madman does something like this," said Thomas's stepfather, Daniel Ding, adding that friends and family were still trying to make sense of the tragedy.

Thomas, his mother, and four siblings came to Canada in 2001 as refugees from Ethiopia who were fleeing pursuing rival tribes in southern Sudan. During their escape from the war-torn country, an exhausted Thomas collapsed. His mother, burdened with getting three more of her children across the border, faced the terrible choice of whether to leave her son behind or to save her other children. She turned back and looked at Thomas sitting there, crying. He would not be left to die.

The family believed life in Edmonton would be peaceful, and Thomas's future looked bright. He was preparing for life as a student at the Northern Alberta Institute of Technology, where he planned to study mechanics. Now his family was thrown into unbearable grief.

"Thomas was a good kid ... It's a great loss," said Michael Dak, who met Thomas in a refugee camp in 1997. "We pray that God will give us the courage to cope with this tragedy."

Dwayne's parents reached out to the victims' families after their son's first court appearance. The couple and their son had moved to Canada from Trinidad about fifteen years earlier. Dwayne was not a troublemaker, said his father, and he had been working with a relative, living in his own apartment in the city's northeast. When the Nelsons heard the news about the shooting, they were frightened. The couple had yet to digest the fact that their son was the man accused of pulling the trigger.

"I want to extend my deepest sympathies to the families involved in this incident. It's a tough situation and we're all really grieving," said Oswald Nelson as his distraught wife clung to his side. "I just want them to know we're feeling their pain."

Dwayne later pleaded not guilty to all charges, sparking a five-week trial. Jurors were told there would not be any witnesses testifying that they saw Dwayne pull the trigger, but that evidence would come from two sources—Jacey's half-brother, Safron Bambury, and Dwayne himself.

Testifying at the trial, Safron told jurors a friend called him the day after the shooting, saying Dwayne wanted to talk to him. He went for a drive with the friend and

Dwayne, who told Safron he was the one who had fatally shot Jacey, who was not only Safron's brother but also his close friend.

"He said, 'I was the one who did it. I shot your brother. I didn't mean to do it. It was a mistake and I'm sorry,'" said Safron, adding he was shocked to learn the news. "He was hurt. He was remorseful. Jacey and him were good friends."

Safron also testified that a drink spilled on him by a woman at the club is what sparked the initial fight on the dance floor. Once the gunfire came to an end, he walked through the club and discovered his brother lying on the floor.

"I said, 'Breathe, Jacey, breathe,' and then he died," Safron said.

Dwayne tried fleeing to Trinidad in the days after the shooting, but he was apprehended by police at the Edmonton International Airport. Homicide Detective Ernie Schreiber spent nearly four hours interviewing Dwayne, who at first gave an endless stream of denials. But then he began answering yes to some of Ernie's questions, admitting he was at the club and was one of the people involved in the fight.

Ernie knew Dwayne was a friend of Jacey's and could clearly see he was affected by the death, afraid of retaliation for his actions that night. Ernie stayed on Dwayne's emotional side, noting how bad it was that his friend was shot and that he didn't believe it was intentional. He also told Dwayne there were security cameras in the area and asked what he thought those cameras would tell police about what happened after he left the club. Eventually Dwayne cracked and asked Ernie how long he could be locked up in jail.

"It was at that point that I knew the tide had turned," said Ernie. "He truly did feel bad about Jacey being dead and being responsible for that. As long as I stayed focused on that and kept bringing that back into the loop, it was a matter of time. He thought he was shooting at the people he was fighting with, but it was a night club. You don't know where the rounds go when they leave the end of the barrel."

Dwayne cried after the confession, repeatedly telling Ernie he was really a good guy.

"I didn't mean to. Everybody knows I didn't mean to," he said in the videotaped interview, adding he only planned to fire one shot. Dwayne also told investigators that after he fled the club, he stopped at 82nd Street and Jasper Avenue to toss the gun as far as he could down an embankment. There had been a fresh dump of snow that weekend, so Ernie thought the weapon would be an easy find. Despite a massive search, the gun was never recovered.

After hearing all the evidence, Dwayne's fate was now in the hands of the jury. Defence lawyer Dino Botto urged members to reject the two separate confessions made by Dwayne, who could have been covering up for the actual shooter and was induced by the police. Dino also argued that the Crown had failed to prove Dwayne was the actual gunman, since not one person in the crowded club had come forward to identify him as the shooter. If the jury did find he was the killer, Dino urged them to bring a verdict of manslaughter rather than second-degree murder, since Dwayne did not intend to kill anyone and was provoked into doing it.

The Crown, however, urged the jury to find Dwayne guilty on all counts, noting he had twice confessed to the deadly crime. Jurors were also told that, despite Dwayne's claim he was a "good man," he did the shooting out of anger and bravado because he was hanging out with the wrong crowd.

After more than three days of deliberations, the six men and six women on the jury found Dwayne guilty of killing the three men and wounding three other people. Some jurors wiped away tears as their recommendations were read before the court. Eight recommended that Dwayne not be eligible for parole for at least ten years, while another recommended fifteen.

More than three years after his deadly crime, Dwayne was sentenced to life in prison with no chance of parole for fifteen years. Court of Queen's Bench Justice Stephen Hillier said the irrational and high-risk violence displayed by Dwayne is the kind of behaviour feared by citizens across Canada. A public shooting such as this undermines the fabric of a civilized society, he added.

Dave's parents flew to Edmonton from Toronto and wept as they read their victim-impact statements before the court. Just three days after he had married his twenty-three-year-old bride in Toronto, Dave drove with two friends to Edmonton, searching for a dream job in the oil-rich

Deodat Persaud holds a photo of his son, Dave Persaud, twenty-one, one of three people shot and killed on October 29, 2006, at the Red Light Lounge. (Photo courtesy of Sun Media)

province. He last spoke to his father just hours before he was fatally shot, telling him that he was planning to attend church in the morning after spending an evening on the town.

Dave was born in Guyana, the family's middle son. He loved cars and planned on opening a business installing automotive electronics while his wife ran a daycare in the basement of their home. The plan was to first earn as much money as possible to launch their dreams.

While waiting for his job to start in the oil patch, Dave worked two jobs at Home Depot and Pizza 73. He had planned to go back to Toronto when his wife finished school in June, then have her move to Edmonton with him, where they'd buy a house with a Jacuzzi. Outside of court, Dave's parents spoke about the pain of losing their son.

"He has shot all of us," said Dave's mother, Jasmatti Persaud. "He has killed all of us, not just Dave, all of us."

The death left Dave's father devastated. "Today I am lost and broken. I have no motivation for life. ...I simply don't care anymore," said Deodat, a pastor. "Sadness has become my friend, my constant companion."

MELISSA JANE LETAIN

On a cold winter night in 1987, Melissa Jane Letain left work, carrying a rose, a card, and a pendant in a plastic bag. It was the eve of Valentine's Day, and the twenty-four-year-old was headed out for a romantic evening with her boyfriend.

Melissa left work at Champs Elysee hair salon in West Edmonton Mall around 9 p.m. and headed for the apartment she shared with her boyfriend at 17744 81st Avenue. The hairstylist took her normal route home along the cement walkway between houses in the area of 87th Avenue and 177th Street, unaware that a predator was stocking her movements.

Lurking in the shadows was a killer, who grabbed Melissa and dragged her to a waiting vehicle, leaving the Valentine's gifts scattered in the snow.

Her co-workers knew something was wrong when the reliable Melissa failed to show up for her 10 a.m. shift the next day. They called her boyfriend to see if they could find her, but he didn't know where she was.

That same day, Melissa's fully clothed body was found seventy-five kilometres southwest of Edmonton under the Genesee bridge on the ice of the North Saskatchewan River—just hours before her sister reported her missing. She had been assaulted, then dumped over the bridge.

The killer used a nylon rope with a hangman's noose and several coils to strangle her. A pair of old pantyhose that didn't belong to Melissa was also found beside her body.

Fourteen-year-old Craig Gordon attended an all-boys private boarding school near the Genesee bridge. The school was known for its strict policies and had a reputation for cleaning up bad behaviour. It was also very outdoor-geared, hosting snowshoe races every year around Valentine's Day.

In the early morning hours of February 14, 1987, Craig set out with his team of six classmates and an alumnus as their guide for the twenty-five-kilometre trek that would take all day to complete. Being a bit of a troublemaker, Craig was goofing around on the Genesee bridge railing when he dropped one of his gloves into the inky darkness below. He would have to wait until the sun rose in order to find it.

When Craig and his group crossed over the bridge on their way back to school later that day, he looked over the railing to see if he could spot his lost glove. There it was, lying in the middle of the ice, along with the body of a young woman.

"From first glance, you could tell that something was seriously wrong with the situation. The way she looked was disturbing," said Craig, noting there was a yellow rope with a pair of pantyhose tied to one end. Other items in garbage bags were strewn around the body.

The rest of the team went back to school as Craig, with the adult chaperone, headed down to the river to try and reach the lifeless woman. On their hands and knees, the pair crawled onto the ice, but it was too soft to support them. There was no way to reach the body, and they decided to call police. Craig had no doubt the woman was already dead.

"It was sickly disturbing," said Craig, who spent the week with his family in Edmonton following the grisly discovery. "I was a wreck. I slept with my sister the whole time when I was home. I had dreams and mind games just playing with my head that the guy saw us or the guy knew it was us that saw the body. I was fortunate to have a father who could sit down with me and say 'as much as it's affecting you, imagine how it's affecting the family of Melissa.'"

Melissa's death sent a chill throughout the city that winter. In less than seven weeks between February and March, three women had disappeared, including Melissa, but police said none of the cases were connected.

Former Mountie Ray Munro was chief of the general investigation unit at the time, in charge of the ten officers hunting for Melissa's killer, who was later profiled as a psychopath. Ray was working on a case outside the country at the time of Melissa's death, and the investigation was well on its way by the time he became involved a month later.

To Ray, it looked like a personal robbery gone wrong. He hoped the hangman's noose used to strangle Melissa would lead police to the killer,

RCMP *Sergeant Ray Munro holds the hangman's noose—made of seven coils of standard yellow nylon rope—that the killer used to strangle and kill Melissa Jane Letain. (Photo courtesy of Sun Media)*

since so few people know how to tie one. Three months later, Ray displayed the noose to the public, hoping the knot would prompt a citizen to contact Crime Stoppers, and it did. Between forty and fifty people called the tip line, with nineteen of those providing useful information that was passed along to the RCMP. "You are hoping that one person that would have knowledge or knows something about it will come forward," Ray said. "It's not that common, that type of knotting," he added. However, Ray stated that the rope and everything else associated with the crime scene could have just been a ploy, an attempt to confuse the manner of death. "It's one of those things you unfortunately don't get the answers [to] until a person's apprehended."

A few of Melissa's belongings were never recovered: a CN keychain with a single key, a woman's gold-tone watch, a blue leather or leather-looking woman's wallet, and a green clutch purse with a gold clasp.

As the investigation progressed, more evidence surfaced about the events that may have unfolded during the moments leading up to the young woman's death. A woman walking home in the same area later told police she became aware of the assault when she heard a groan or gurgling sound. She turned and saw a man clutching a woman and hushing her to be quiet before she was dragged away.

A friend of the witness told a newspaper reporter that the witness didn't see the woman's face, but the winter clothing—a long coat and high boots—matched what police told her Melissa was known to be wearing. The friend said the man looked up and stared at the witness, leading her to believe he was studying her features. It was the last time Melissa was seen alive. "She literally shakes every time she starts talking about it," said the witness's friend.

Following the report, investigators combed the footpath and park areas where the attack took place. But the search turned up nothing, and a search for other witnesses in the area also failed to generate any new leads.

Police later confirmed the witnessed assault was linked to Melissa's abduction. A profile of the suspect was released, describing him as six feet tall with dark hair swept back at the sides, and a slim-to-medium build. He was wearing a blue-and-white coat with dark pants at the time.

Melissa Jane Letain, twenty-four, was last seen February 13, 1987, leaving a popular West Edmonton Mall hair salon, where she worked as a stylist. (Photo courtesy of Sun Media)

"I would love to tell you that we had someone hot and heavy and [that we have] conspired as to how we could catch him," said Ray, who worked fourteen years in the homicide units in both Edmonton and Calgary. The circumstances of the case indicated to Ray that it was a random or chance crime, given where it occurred. With advances in science and DNA technologies, however, Ray believes the case can be solved if the right evidence comes along, even though it's been more than twenty-seven years.

"In those days we didn't have DNA [matching tools]," he said. "So yeah, there was always hope at that time that science was going to advance to a [point where we could] specifically identify suspects. ... It's still an active and open investigation. At any time, you could get a lead. People don't forget and have come forward many years later with something that was bothering them, something they heard or something they saw that has led to valuable suspects," added Ray, now sixty-six years old. The case stuck with him throughout his career, along with other murders that have gone unsolved for decades.

"All the ones that are unsolved I remember, just because they are a major part of your own personal life. You are working on them all the time, years in some cases. You are frustrated because you can't get that one piece of evidence to actually identify a suspect, and it bothers you that something like that could occur without having the strings attached to the person responsible. So you try harder and you work longer."

Corporal Rick Jane with the RCMP historical homicide unit is now the lead investigator on Melissa's file. He's still waiting for the missing link that could finally lead police to the killer.

"Unsolved homicides are often solved when a member of the public who has information about the murder makes the decision to come forward to police and provide that information," said Rick. "Some unsolved [crimes] are solved due to advances in forensic science, and the RCMP continues to evaluate potential forensic testing as new technology emerges."

LIFE IN THE HOMICIDE UNIT

I t was around 2 a.m. when Edmonton Homicide Detective Paul Gregory was woken from a deep sleep by a call from one of his colleagues about a possible murder. Shortly after midnight, the body of a twenty-two-year-old man was discovered in the city's north end, lying next to a vehicle in an alley behind Bayview Manor apartments near 131st Avenue and 69th Street. The man had been shot, leading police to believe they were dealing with Edmonton's forty-third murder victim of 2011. The city had already broken its previous record of thirty-nine homicides, set in 2005, and was on pace to become the homicide capital of Canada for the second time in six years.

Paul knew it was his turn to be the primary detective on a homicide case. It was his first time leading an investigation, and the thirty-nine-year-old was a nervous wreck.

"The moment that phone rang, my heart just sunk into my stomach. I knew right away," said Paul, who, at the time, had been an Edmonton Police Service (EPS) member for ten years, and a homicide detective for the previous two-and-a-half years.

"The next thing you know your phone is ringing off the hook. You are directing people to do things as you drive into the office and doing up your tie at the same time. There are a hundred million questions going through your head."

How many witnesses are there? What resources are available? Is the scene contained? What needs to be done? These are just a few of the questions swirling through Paul's mind after receiving the call. Once he reaches the office, the pace picks up even more, and he's faced with an abundance of important decisions as six detectives wait for him to call the shots in the investigation.

The first ones to arrive at a homicide are the patrol cops, who tape off the area to preserve any evidence, move people away from the scene, and identify any witnesses to be sent to police headquarters for interviews. Wearing suits and ties, and often holding large coffees, the homicide detectives, along with the forensics team, pick up where the front-line officers left off.

By the time the detectives arrive, forensics team members, dressed in white jump suits from head to toe, are already there collecting evidence from the scene. The mood is serious. The smell of death fills the air. It's a smell that Homicide Detective Carlos Cardoso has come to know well.

"It's hard to describe. [But] when you go [to a scene], you always know that smell," said forty-three-year-old Carlos, an EPS member for more than nineteen years, and a homicide detective for three-and-a-half. "Your first sudden death—you'll always remember that smell. It will stay with you. It's not pleasant."

The first forty-eight hours following a slaying are the most crucial. Detectives become slaves to the investigation, working twenty hours the first day and sometimes staying up for thirty-six hours in order to get in front of the investigation before it gets in front of them. Birthday parties, holidays, weekend plans with the family are suddenly put on hold. Paul is on the phone constantly. The file is always going through his head.

"Even when you are sitting at home and you just finished a fifteen-, sixteen-hour day, you have [the] family calling you or witnesses calling you," he said. "You let the adrenalin take you as long as you can go, and then after that you are in survival mode. You have to do it; you have no choice."

Sometimes it's easy to catch the killer, but sometimes it doesn't happen at all. If there is no suspect, police explore different avenues, such as going to the media, making a public appeal for help with the family, installing wire taps, or starting an undercover project, depending on the file. Witnesses are interviewed—some are cooperative, some aren't. Sometimes detectives hit a wall and need a break in the case in order to move forward. Other times they are close to making an arrest but just need one more piece of the puzzle.

"It's frustrating. None of us want to see a file not get solved," said Carlos. "At the end of the day you are working for the family, you are working for the victim, and if we can't bring closure for a family, it's hard to take."

Fortunately, Carlos and Paul have often brought a degree of closure to families struck with grief over the loss of a loved one. Recently, Paul had had the opportunity to tell a B.C. woman that an arrest had been made in the death of her thirty-one-year-old son, assaulted outside a downtown bar during his first weekend living in Edmonton. It's moments like this that keep Paul, Carlos, and other detectives in the homicide unit pushing themselves to the limit in order to make sure that justice is served.

"It was pretty satisfying. You could hear literally the excitement in her voice," said Paul about delivering news of the arrest to the man's mother. "All the other times I have spoken with her, she had been defeated. To hear that glimmer of excitement in her voice, it was refreshing, absolutely."

In the corner of Homicide Staff Sergeant Bill Clark's office sits a sign posted on the end of a wooden stake that reads "Bill Clark for Mayor."

"The sign was found by Detective Sharon Bach in a little town between Penticton and Kelowna," says the fifty-two-year-old, who was born and raised in Edmonton's north side. "I laughed. I thought it was great. I thought, [the town] couldn't handle a Bill Clark for mayor."

A large map of the city hangs on the wall near Bill's desk, but it rarely gets used since he knows the streets like the back of his hand. The rest of the homicide unit at Edmonton police headquarters looks like a typical office one would find in a high-rise downtown. A few flat-screen televisions and whiteboards line the large room that is filled with the desks and computers where detectives spend countless hours filling out mountains of paperwork and reports up to two hundred pages long. It's where nineteen homicide detectives and two cold cases detectives spend much of their time when they're not out searching for killers. Another five detectives were assigned to join the team over the next few months to help with the spike in homicides in 2011.

At the back of the room is a bookshelf housing several large binders with the names of homicide victims on the labels. These are the unsolved files, said Bill, and they are a thorn in every detective's side.

"We know who did this one, we know who did this one," said Bill, as he pointed to various binders. There's just not enough evidence to lay a charge.

Outside the office, in the hallway, a small light with the word "quiet" dimly glows on the ceiling. This is where the interview rooms are located—a place where detectives question witnesses and grill potential suspects linked to a crime. One room is the soft interview room, explains Bill; it has a black leather couch on which guests can sit and relax. The other small interview room near the holding cells isn't as comfy. It has only two chairs—one for a detective and one for the suspect. Bill demonstrates how he likes to pull the chair as close to the suspect as possible, sometimes touching the suspect's knees. It's an uncomfortable place for a bad guy, but it's a place where Bill shines.

"I love to interview the bad guy. Interviewing the bad guy is just a game," said Bill, his eyes lighting up as he talks about some of his interrogations. "It's just him and me. My job is to get the confession, and he obviously doesn't want to tell me what he did."

Getting a killer to confess can take hours. On a Sunday night in October 2008, Bill was getting ready to go home and rest after a long day at the office, when out of the blue an aspiring filmmaker, twenty-nine-year-old Mark Twitchell, was brought into police headquarters for questioning.

Previously unknown to police, Twitchell was a suspect in the killing and dismembering of thirty-eight-year-old Johnny Altinger, who was lured to a rented garage in Mill Woods under the impression he would be meeting a woman he had met online. Instead of experiencing a romantic encounter, Johnny was attacked with a pipe, stabbed, and dismembered; his remains were dumped down a sewer in an alley off 129th Avenue and 86th Street.

Running on adrenalin, Bill spent the next six hours questioning Twitchell until 6 a.m. At first he played the role of "good cop," listening to Twitchell's web of lies. Then came Bill's "bad cop" routine, and Twitchell began to sweat.

"I knew the whole time he was telling me he was a liar, but I'm just sitting there smiling and letting him fill me up with all the lies. I've had some excellent liars. Some people get mad at you, some people stand right up and yell at you," said Bill.

For the EPS veteran, there's no better feeling than putting a bad guy behind bars. It's an adrenalin rush that fills the whole office with excitement. "Ultimately we want to get the bad guy," adds Bill. "We do whatever we can."

"There's no doubt I thrive on it. I love the work, I love the files, I love the whole part of the investigation. Homicide's a unique brand. It's a different breed. Those detectives are dedicated people. The guys in our unit continually go hard."

In June 2011, Bill Clark began to worry. It was only six months into the year and twenty-four people had already been murdered, putting a big strain on the fourteen members then in the Edmonton Police homicide unit. The detectives didn't know it yet, but that year they would have to contend with a record-breaking forty-eight homicides.

"We realized we were going to be overwhelmed," said Bill. "It was just murder after murder. We were running crazy. There never seemed to be a break."

With summer holidays coming up, the unit had no choice but to go to upper management and ask for help. In response, they were given ten detectives from other departments within the service to help with the ballooning workload, but the murders didn't stop.

One week in July 2011 was particularly busy for Bill and the rest of the squad. At around 10:20 p.m. on July 24, neighbours in the Brintnell community found twenty-six-year-old Michael Wayne Tunnicliffe lying on the ground suffering from a gunshot wound. Two days later, Eric Larry

Cardinal was stabbed to death during a fight at an inner-city park, just a stone's throw from the Edmonton Remand Centre downtown. During the next two days, two more slayings were recorded, bringing the death toll to thirty-three. The files piled up on Bill's desk, leaving him and the rest of the unit in disbelief.

"We just said, 'another one? Are you kidding me? What is with this city?' We were just amazed with how many we were getting," said Bill, noting detectives didn't believe the trend would continue, but it did.

"We've had those times where we've had two or three in a week, but then you get a break. [But these] just seemed to be coming every week."

In June 2011, Rod Knecht left his position in Ottawa as the RCMP's senior deputy commissioner and came to Edmonton to fill the shoes as the city's top cop. With the

Staff Sergeant Bill Clark (left) of the Edmonton Police homicide unit chats with detectives Carlos Cardoso (centre) and Paul Gregory at downtown police headquarters in June 2012. (Photo by Perry Mah / Courtesy of Sun Media)

soaring homicide rate now the talk of the town, Rod knew he was in for a challenge. All eyes were on him to come up with a plan.

Two months after his arrival, Rod revealed a violence-reduction strategy aimed to reduce the frequency and severity of violent crime in Edmonton. He said the detailed plan would be a marathon, not a sprint, and pointed out there would be no simple solutions to end the bloodshed.

The killings not only inspired fear among some city residents, but also highlighted some of the social problems in Edmonton's most troubled neighbourhoods. Part of Rod's plan involved putting more officers on the streets of those neighbourhoods. Since many of the killings involved knives, Rod met with the Crown prosecutor's office to discuss options for leveraging federal Criminal Code legislation to address edged weapons.

With no common pattern or single cause or factor in the mounting death toll, Chief Knecht kept his fingers crossed that the year was just an anomaly.

"We are seeing no discernible pattern whatsoever. That's a little bit frustrating for us because we have to spread resources all over the place instead of focusing on one area," said Rod at the time, adding that his plan to reduce the violence could take up to five years to implement.

"I came in at an unfortunate time, when the homicides were at the top of the list and the people were telling me, you have to develop a homicide strategy," he said.

One year into the plan, Chief Knecht was pleased to reveal that violent crime was down by 4.6 per cent and homicides had dropped by about 56 per cent. He pointed out that about 60 per cent of the homicides in 2011 involved the city's most vulnerable—the homeless, addicted, and mentally ill, a population police continue to focus on to make sure they get the appropriate services and stay out of trouble.

Due to the number of cases piling up in 2011, detectives were often forced to put aside what they were working on to take on a new file, but the lower number of homicides the following year allowed them to return to those files and make sure they didn't turn cold.

"They are never forgotten. You just have to get back to them and dedicate the resources," said Bill, who can't count how many times he's been woken at 2:30 a.m. by a homicide call. With more than ten years in the unit, his mind automatically clicks on and goes into overdrive.

Detective Carlos Cardoso had no idea how exhausting 2011 was until it was over. Between June and July, he had a day-and-a-half off. The rest of the days turned into a blur. Looking back, Carlos describes the year as a mess. If it wasn't for those additional officers, he doesn't know how the homicide detectives would have been able to keep up.

"I really didn't know where the year went. It just flew by. Some days you just kind of lost track of what day of the week it was," said Carlos. "We just adapted. At one point we were almost laughing because we thought, really? Again? But you make it work."

THE "PUNKY" CASE AND DNA

At six years old, Corrine Gustavson knew how to wrap her mother around her pinky finger. Her cute little smile and laugh were a part of her charm and usually helped her get whatever she wanted. Her charm was one of the things Karen Vallette remembers about the daughter she was only beginning to know.

Karen was at her father's place one morning during the Labour Day long weekend in September 1992 when she received a phone call from her husband that Corrine, nicknamed "Punky" due to her wild sprouts of blonde, spiky hair, had been snatched from the front yard of the couple's home in the Abbotsfield neighbourhood of northeast Edmonton. The child had been playing with her five-year-old friend, who ran back to her house and told her mother, "A murderer took Corinne!" Filled with worry and fear, Karen rushed home immediately to begin searching for her missing child. "I just wanted to find her. I just thought she'd come home," she said.

But Punky didn't come home, sparking a massive city-wide search for the happy little girl. Two days later, hope of finding Punky alive turned into tragedy when her tiny, shoeless body was found lying face down between a number of large trucks and trailers in the gravel of a Sherwood Park trucking yard. The child had been brutally raped, smothered, and left for dead. It was news that shook the entire city to its core.

"It was so sad," said Punky's mother. "I just wanted to go out there and catch the guy and kill him."

The girl's brutal slaying was devastating for her family. The couple's marriage eventually broke up, and Punky's father spiraled into a deep depression. He'd been caring for her the morning she disappeared and had only been distracted for a moment.

Footprints from a cleated shoe were found in the gravel where the body was found, as well as near the scene of the abduction. The tread was specific to the Mitre brand of baseball cleats. Forensics investigators also found tire tracks in the trucking yard and made casts of them, suspecting they were from the killer's vehicle, which they figured was a mid-sized front-wheel drive.

Terry Alm had been a detective with the Edmonton Police homicide unit for only a few months when he was assigned the job of being the primary investigator in the case. The unit was given a heads-up that the file could be turned over to them shortly after Punky disappeared.

Terry had two small children himself at the time—ages seven and five. Even though he had previously worked in the sex crimes and child abuse unit, investigating the violent murder of a child was another story.

"I don't know how you ever really prepare yourself for something like that," said Terry. "You do the job because that's what you do, but it's always different when there's a child involved. [This] was tough on everyone."

Terry and the rest of the detectives assigned to the case soon became overwhelmed with the number of tips flooding in. Approximately forty to fifty investigators were now working on the file, where there was always something to do. The investigation was the largest in Edmonton police history, resulting in 5,100 tips and four hundred suspects. After a while, Terry couldn't tell a good tip from a bad one. There were so many rumours going around that some of the tips took on a life of their own.

"There was always work to be done. There were always new tips. It was never one of those cases that was shelved and then looked at. It was an active case even after I left it," said Terry. "We were getting phone calls from everybody, saying you should come look at this guy or this guy. The door-to-doors became tips themselves. We had all these detectives scouring that area for months. Everyone's entitled to their own opinion, but when you don't have hard evidence to either substantiate or support someone as a suspect or eliminate someone, it's somewhat frustrating. At the end of the day, I felt like we needed forensics to really help us out."

In the years that followed, Terry waited patiently for advancements in DNA technology and did what he could to move the investigation forward in the mean time. A lot of work was done on a pubic hair that was found on the heal of Punky's sock, and some good suspects were profiled over the years, but police needed more to solidify evidence about the actual killer.

In January 2000, detectives sent the evidence they had to a lab in North Carolina to be re-examined. One year later, Terry received a phone call from one of the scientists, delivering the news he had been waiting for. They had an offender profile. All they needed was to find a match.

"That was probably one of the best days of my policing career. Then, of course, I had to work towards making sure that profile could be entered into the Canadian DNA data bank," said Terry, who left Edmonton Police in 2002.

"I wouldn't have stayed in homicide as long as I did, but because of the Punky case [I stayed]. I wanted to try and bring it to some kind of a resolution and successful conclusion as best I could. When we got the DNA in the data bank, that was when I said: 'Okay, we're way ahead of where we were a few years ago, I can now leave homicide.'"

Clifford Sleigh always had a peculiar habit of wearing baseball cleats. Little did he know, that habit—along with his DNA—would someday earn him a first-degree murder conviction, thanks to advancements in DNA technology. The evidence collected from the crime scene that was sent to the lab in North Carolina—such as Punky's underwear and swabs taken from her private areas—allowed scientists to complete an offender profile, which was then entered into Canada's National DNA Data Bank.

Sleigh was already behind bars, serving a fifteen-year prison sentence for the rapes of two teenaged girls in the years following Punky's death. Due to his past convictions, a court-ordered sample of his DNA was taken in December 2002. That DNA profile was entered into the DNA data bank and resulted in a match with the offender profile that had been developed in North Carolina. The chances of that occurring randomly were estimated between one in 25 trillion and one in 640 trillion.

Sleigh was sentenced to life in prison with no chance of parole for twenty-five years for taking Punky's young life. Why did he choose the charming girl with the spiky blonde hair? He was angry with his common-law wife, he later said, so he headed out to rape a girl he knew. Unable to find her, he spotted Punky and grabbed her because she was the child closest to the fence. Sleigh maintains she was still alive when he left her bloodied body in the trucking yard.

By the time Sleigh was charged for his horrific crime it had been ten years, three months, and thirteen days since Punky's death. After so many years filled with sorrow, that day on which Sleigh was charged was one that finally had some happiness. It was also one her mother will never forget.

"I was working at the Dollar Store and one of the detectives called me and asked if we could meet. I knew exactly that they had caught the man," she said. "I just hung up the phone and told my boss I would be back. I was shaking. It was coming to the end now." Punky's mother never gave up hope the killer would be caught, even though so much time had passed. The little girl she barely got to know was still in her thoughts every day.

"I knew they were going to catch the guy sooner or later. In a way I feel like I have closure, but in a way I don't. He's still alive and doing time, but he still has the right to go to school. He didn't give my daughter a chance to go to school, so why should we pay for him to be in jail? It's just not fair."

Corinne "Punky" Gustavson. The six-year-old was abducted and murdered in September 1992 by Clifford Sleigh. (Photo courtesy of Sun Media)

Terry had been retired from the Edmonton Police Service for about ten months when he got the call from detectives still working on the case. Between four hundred and five hundred samples of DNA from suspects or persons of interests had been submitted to the crime lab for comparison against the suspect's DNA, and Terry had been hopeful it would only be a matter of time before he would get the call.

"They asked me if I was sitting down," said Terry, who then went back and helped the Edmonton Police and the Crown prosecutor for two years while the case worked its way through the courts.

"It was quite rewarding at the end, especially since I was quite close with the family. I'm still in touch with them, so it was rewarding from that perspective to bring closure to them," Terry added.

The scientists and technicians working at the RCMP forensics lab in Edmonton help put killers like Sleigh behind bars. The lab is one of three RCMP forensic labs operating across Canada. Inside, approximately fifty-five employees work on DNA analysis, toxicology, tracing evidence, anti-counterfeiting, firearms, and tool mark identification.

In Ottawa, the National DNA Data Bank (NDDB), created in June of 2000, also assists law enforcement agencies by identifying or eliminating suspects, or determining whether or not a serial offender is involved, through processing and analyzing DNA samples.

Under the DNA Identification Act (1998), all those convicted of serious crimes, such as murder and sexual assault, must give a sample of their DNA. Some of those convicted prior to the act becoming legislation—such as dangerous offenders and murderers who killed at least two different times—must also submit a sample. For those convicted of less serious offences, such as assault, it's up to the Crown to make a request for a sample, which then may be ordered at a judge's discretion. Once collected, offenders' DNA profiles are then matched against thousands of unknown DNA samples from unsolved crimes across the country.

In 1989, an Ottawa rapist became the first in Canada to be convicted because of DNA matching technology. His sixty-eight-year-old victim had picked him out of a police lineup, but he denied any involvement in the crime. After samples of his hair, blood, and saliva were taken, DNA tests linked the man to the semen found on the victim's nightgown and bedspread, leading to his arrest. In court, the rapist suddenly changed his plea to guilty after the judge ruled the DNA evidence admissible. He was sentenced to seven years behind bars.

In Edmonton, the historical homicide unit has had one conviction using the NDDB and another case that went to trial.

DNA technology has proved to be a useful tool to help put killers behind bars, but it has also been used to free people from jail who've been wrongly convicted. In 1969, at the age of sixteen, David Milgaard was convicted for the murder of Saskatoon nursing aid Gail Miller. Milgaard spent twenty-three years in prison until the Supreme Court overturned his conviction in 1992. DNA evidence helped catch the real killer, Larry Fisher, who was convicted in 1999. For the time he wrongly spent behind bars, Milgaard was awarded $10 million.

The Norwood neighbourhood in north-central Edmonton doesn't have a reputation of being the safest community in the city. Filled with a mixture of older homes and affordable housing, the area has seen its share of serious and petty crime. Signs stating the community does not tolerate prostitution line some of the streets boasting homes with chain-link fences draped around the front yard. Despite its problems, however, Lillian Berube called the neighbourhood home.

Tired of living in a flood zone by the North Saskatchewan River, Lillian and her husband decided to move to a quaint bungalow at 11630 90th Street in Norwood, where the childless couple quickly warmed to neighbours. Lillian continued to live at the home after her husband passed away, and she eventually became known in the community as everybody's grandmother.

"She was extremely independent. She did everything herself at her ripe old age—gardening, yard maintenance," said Kim Robinson, who had lived next door to Lillian since 1979. "I chatted with her lots. She was just a really nice little old lady."

On the evening of August 27, 1987, an intruder broke into Lillian's home. When the eighty-three-year-old came upon the unknown man, he repeatedly punched and viciously kicked her into unconsciousness in her kitchen. The thug went on a rampage, swiping the senior's cash and jewelry, before ransacking other rooms in the house. He also smashed the natural gas meter in Lillian's basement with a hammer or ashtray, and took a claw hammer to the furnace's chimney pipe, leaving the tool embedded in it.

"We're not really sure if it was an attempt to burn the place or just someone fuming in a fit of anger," Homicide Detective Tom Peebles said at the time, adding it was the most disgusting attack he had ever seen. Police also found a distinctive earring inside Lillian's home, which was either dropped or pulled off during the struggle.

Lillian lay on her kitchen floor until morning, when a neighbour came to check on her after noticing that the drapes of the home hadn't been moved—a secret signal the two women used to let each other know everything was okay. Suffering from severe neck injuries, a fractured jaw, and broken ribs, Lillian managed to drag her tiny body to the screen door in the kitchen to let her neighbour inside. Although she was conscious and sitting on the floor, she couldn't remember what happened.

Lillian was taken to hospital and died six days later from cardiac arrest. An autopsy revealed she suffered a concussion, facial and rib fractures, and bruises from the assault. The injuries were a contributing factor to her death.

"It was very, very sad. This guy apparently noticed her taking money out of the bank and then entered the house and demanded it," said Lillian's nephew, Jim Want, who saw his aunt two to three times a year at family get-togethers.

"She was a very nice lady. It was a big shock," he added. "Nobody could think of anybody who would have any reason to wrong Aunt Lill. It was really upsetting to my mother because they were great friends as well as being sisters."

The case went unsolved for twenty-two years, leaving the family with little hope the killer would ever be found. Detectives were also stumped, later offering a $40,000 reward for information leading to the killer. Based on information gathered during the investigation, police believed Lillian's attacker was nineteen to twenty years old, and Aboriginal with shoulder-length black hair. They thought he lived in the area and was motivated to commit a robbery, since he left the house with a wedding ring, other jewelry, and some cash. But that's all they had—until November 2009 when new life was breathed into the case thanks to DNA.

During the struggle, Lillian managed to grab a tuft of hair from her attacker. In 2001 a DNA sample was obtained from that hair and its profile placed in the National DNA Data Bank. It took eight years until a hit. The hair was matched to forty-one-year-old Charles William Abou, who was already serving time in a B.C. prison. He was subsequently charged with second-degree murder.

Detective Howie Antoniuk of the Edmonton Police historical homicide unit delivered the shocking news to Lillian's family. The case had become one of the oldest homicides ever to be cracked in the city.

"It's almost as emotional for us as it is for the family," Howie said. "They've been waiting for some closure all of these years, so they [are] quite emotional and excited. Watching their reaction, *you* get kind of emotional," he added.

Although a DNA match had been made, putting the rest of the pieces together wasn't a simple task. It took police close to a year and a half to gather everything they needed and finally lay charges. Once the suspect was identified, detectives spent hours wading through and tracking down old documents, and researching police files in the archives. Even though they had the DNA, they still had to prove it was criminally significant before going after the suspect.

"It's almost like a treasure hunt in a sense, but it does get very draining," Howie said. "[But] once we got on his trail, it was a chase [and] there was that excitement there putting it all together.

"We basically take his life from the day he was born to the day we charged him. We go back through all his criminal history and records, and we basically know him better than he knows himself."

According to Howie, the original investigators were very close to Abou's trail. They went and looked at all the people charged with break and enters in the general area—a task Howie described as a massive undertaking. Police, however, stopped their search about ten blocks away from where Abou was committing his crimes.

Howie's unit receives a lot of DNA samples, but many of them aren't criminally significant so detectives can't act upon them. A scenario he gave as an example is that of a crime scene at a house party, where there could be hundreds of DNA samples taken, but investigators can't put anything to anybody. In the Lillian Berube case, however, it was obvious that the tuft of hair did not belong to the senior.

"It was a pretty significant piece of DNA, [which] is rare. If it wasn't for the DNA we wouldn't have got anybody for it," said Howie, adding cases such as Lillian's give hope to other families waiting for closure. But he cautions, "Everybody thinks because we have DNA, it's the be-all, end-all. It's not that simple."

At the time of the savage attack, Abou was bumming around Edmonton with no fixed address. Parole board documents show he had more than forty-five criminal convictions on his record, including three assaults. The other offences were mostly property related.

Abou had a history of breaking into homes while they were occupied. In two cases, he entered houses that were lived in by women. Abou also struggled with drug and alcohol addiction, which included the use of heroin and crack cocaine. He moved to Vancouver's notorious downtown east side in the 1990s, contracted HIV, and in prison had himself been the victim of numerous assaults.

At the time the murder charge was laid, Abou was serving a two-year sentence for drug possession and break and enter. At some point he had been ordered to submit a DNA sample as part of a sentencing. It was that order which ultimately linked him to Lillian's murder.

In August 2010, Abou was handed a thirteen-year prison sentence after pleading guilty to manslaughter and break and enter with intent. During the sentencing hearing, the court heard that a drunken Abou broke into Lillian's home through an unlocked rear door. Three victim impact statements were also read to the court. Lillian's relatives spoke of recalling the "horror and misery" of the crime and the "devastating effect" it had on the whole family.

Jim Want was one of several family members who gathered in court to watch the proceedings and have a look at his aunt's killer in the flesh. For the first time in years, the family finally felt some closure.

"It was a long time coming," Jim said. "I'm glad they found him before he killed somebody else. I don't think any of us expected they would ever find him," he added. "It was quite amazing that it took so many years and so many advancements in DNA testing to find the fellow. It is absolutely incredible."

Still living next to Lillian's former home, Kim Robinson can't help but think sometimes about the brutal attack on the neighbour he had grown so fond of. Like Lillian's family, he hoped the murder would be solved, but as time passed he doubted it ever would. Now he, too, has closure.

"We have closure, but at the same time closure at what price, really?" he said. "It's just a sad incident that should never have happened."

CHARLOTTE BAAS

Terri Baas can't help but wonder what her eldest daughter's wedding would have been like or how many grandchildren she would have had to spoil.

It's been over thirty years since the life of her daughter, Charlotte, was cut short by the hands of a killer in a deadly fire. That killer has yet to be brought to justice, leaving a dark hole in Terri's life that will never be filled.

"That hole is always there. It gets smaller as time goes by, but I do miss her," said Terri, now sixty-seven. "Her life was just beginning and it was snuffed out."

In the early morning hours of December 18, 1983, emergency crews were called to a fire at 106th Avenue and 151st Street in west Edmonton. There, they found Charlotte dead inside the small, quaint bungalow where she had been living with some friends. The eighteen-year-old was in her bed with a dead dog curled up beside her. An investigation revealed the fire had been intentionally set using gasoline. Charlotte died from carbon monoxide poisoning.

The previous evening, Charlotte had been at her parents' home to celebrate her father Allan's birthday. Terri wanted Charlotte to spend the night so she could cook a big roast dinner the next day and feed her daughter a good hearty meal. Charlotte, however, was adamant she should return home to watch over another teenage girl plus the dogs. Around midnight, Allan gave her a ride home. It was the last time he would see his daughter.

"When he got home he said, 'I don't know why I said good-bye. Normally I say good night,'" Terri recalled.

While Allan was away helping people get their vehicles started in the cold the next day, a homicide detective showed up at the Baas residence to deliver the grim news about their daughter. Terri was home with Charlotte's younger sister at the time. Hearing the news was mortifying.

"I think I just hit the floor. I couldn't believe it," said Terri. "You see [things like this] on TV and ... you think it's not going to hit you, but it can hit you."

Charlotte was identified by dental records, which saved the family the pain of identifying her remains. But never seeing Charlotte again was a harsh reality that was too painful for members of her family to handle.

"My mother wanted to [see her] and the funeral director said, 'No you don't want to see her in this state,'" said Terri. "I didn't want to see the charred remains and have that as a constant memory. I wanted to remember her as she was."

Life for Terri and her family hasn't been easy since Charlotte's untimely death. Allan and Terri divorced four years later. Terri has kept as busy as possible, allowing her to move forward and not dwell too much on the past. She found the strength to pull through her darkest times with the support of a minister, who also happened to be her boss and gave her as much time off as she needed while she mourned the loss of her child.

Charlotte was the older of two girls born fourteen months and twenty days apart. She was an animal lover with a zest for life, a love of nature, and a willingness to try almost anything new. A friend of Charlotte's remembers her beautiful smile and describes her as someone worth knowing.

"She had a good heart and always respected people. Her eyes would shine when she smiled. She liked smiling, I think. She never wanted to hurt anybody and tried to be friendly to everyone," said the friend. "She was intelligent and thoughtful. She also had a bit of a wild side and liked to let loose every once in a while. Char was a wonderful person who never deserved this."

Terri harbours much anger as she continues to wait for answers to her long list of questions about the murder. Throughout the years, she's heard conflicting stories about her daughter's death. One involves someone who was out to get even with another person, but got the wrong house. Terri said police have had suspects in the case, but they never amounted to any arrests.

Some of Terri's anger stems from her feeling that the case was overshadowed by other high-profile murder investigations going on at the time and that not enough attention was spent on the hunt for Charlotte's killer. Although much time has passed, she remains hopeful that whoever killed her daughter will eventually step forward or slip up and tell the wrong person.

"We all have to be accountable for our actions," she said. "I am hoping that maybe it will come to a conclusion." Terri added that the passing of time has helped, somewhat. "The weight is not so heavy on the shoulders, but you still wish that [the one responsible] would be caught."

A $40,000 reward for information leading to the arrest and conviction of the person responsible is still posted in the case. With the hope that reward money might breathe new life into homicide investigations that have sat unsolved on shelves for decades, a staggering $1.24 million remains up for grabs. The idea behind reward money is that it might induce members of the public to bring information forward when all other avenues have been exhausted.

As of 2011, Edmonton Police had thirty-one cold cases, each with a $40,000 reward for those who may be holding the missing piece of the puzzle. Some of the murders on the list are drug and gang-related; some victims were simply in the wrong place at the wrong time.

When selecting for which cases reward money will be offered, an investigator determines the value on a file-by-file basis. Rewards typically range between $10,000 and $40,000 and are reviewed every three years. Some cases, such as that of Karen Ewanciw (see pages 8–15), have been renewed more than five times.

The burned-out home in which Charlotte Hazel Baas was found dead on December 18, 1983. (Photo by Gary Bartlett / Courtesy of Sun Media)

Deputy Police Chief Darryl da Costa didn't recall any rewards being paid out in recent history, but that doesn't mean the offer of reward money hasn't been an effective tool.

"I think it's always helpful to be able to raise the awareness of the crime in the community," he said. "It gives us an opportunity to get more information even if it doesn't lead to an arrest."

As the years pass by with no arrests, Detective Howie Antoniuk with the Edmonton Police historical homicide unit has seen many victims' families struggle to find closure. Some people spiral out of control into substance abuse, and some withdraw from society. Others soldier on, maintaining the hope that some day closure will come. Until that day comes, however, Howie maintains that every cold case is open, waiting to be solved with the right information.

"Our hope is we solve all these crimes, and we work diligently to do that," he said.

MARIE GOUDREAU

At first it was shock, followed by disbelief. Then a pain so deep he wouldn't wish it upon his own worst enemy. Nothing can ever bring back Daniel Goudreau's younger sister, Marie. But even after thirty-six years he hadn't given up hope that the person who abducted his innocent sibling from a quiet country road and left her body in a ditch will some day pay for the heinous crime.

"You are always thinking what could have been, or if she was still alive what she would have done with her life. It never goes away," said Daniel, who thinks about his sister several times a month. He was twenty-five, married, and had already moved off the family homestead when his parents called to tell him Marie was missing.

"It was shock. I couldn't believe it. I thought maybe they had made a mistake or something. You always hope for the best and hope they are wrong about that."

Marie worked at a coffee shop in Edmonton's Southgate Mall and always drove the same route home to her family's farm near Beaumont—a French town located amid sprawling farmers' fields on the prairies just south of the city. The seventeen-year-old was among five of the eight children in the family still living on the farm.

On the night of August 2, 1976, Marie left a friend's house around 10:30 p.m., but she never made it home.

Police knew something was wrong when they found Marie's blue 1972 Plymouth Cricket abandoned on a rural road now known as Ellerslie Road. Parked on an angle, it was still running with the headlights on and had been for more than an hour. The driver's side door was open with the window partly rolled down. Marie's purse containing $20 cash was left undisturbed on the front seat. Her jacket and shoes were also still in the car.

Between 10:50 p.m. and 11:00 p.m., witnesses reported seeing a truck idling nearby at the intersection of Range Road 244 and Township Road 510 just west of Beaumont. Police believe somebody flagged down Marie, possibly pretending to be broken down on the side of the road. When Marie stopped and got out of the car, she was abducted.

"It's very odd. Marie was not known to be picking up hitchhikers. The fact the car was parked in that manner was very curious. It's almost as if she pulled over to speak with someone she viewed as friendly," said RCMP Corporal Ken Beard, who worked tirelessly on the case for about a year during his time with the major crimes unit in Edmonton, from 2008 to 2009. The bulk of the original investigation was done in the late 1970s to early 1980s. Ken's job was to see if any stones had been left unturned.

"She wasn't in a dangerous place. She didn't lead a risky lifestyle," he said. "She was a good girl from a very strong Christian background, and she got caught up in a situation where she was taken advantage of. That doesn't sit well with anybody."

Marie's disappearance sent waves of shock and disbelief throughout her family. They began to wonder and worry what could have happened, still hoping for the best while trying to maintain some normalcy operating the farm.

"All kinds of things go through your head. What could have happened? What can we do to help? But, unfortunately, there wasn't too much anybody could do at that point," Daniel said.

Two days after Marie vanished, her nude body was found in a water-filled ditch about three kilometres north of the town of Devon, southwest of Edmonton. She had been strangled. The news was overwhelming for the Goudreau family.

"It was just awful. Your worst fears were realized. It was pretty traumatic," said Daniel, adding the family had to identify the body—something nobody should ever have to do.

Of Marie's murder, Daniel added, "We thought it would be solved soon and we were hoping it would have been. You are always thinking some person [might do] this again and you certainly don't want that to happen. It's one of those nagging feelings that you just don't know how to handle."

Some DNA was obtained from the crime scene, but police weren't able to link it to anyone in particular. Ken believes that one day there might be an opportunity for a match, but whether or not the suspect is still alive is anybody's guess. At one time, the prime suspect was a man by the name of Gary McAstocker, who had been working for an Edmonton-based moving company, but Ken said McAstocker committed suicide, creating a loose end.

"We would hear from time to time rumours about it being this person or that person, but nothing [was] confirmed," said Daniel. "You [had] to trust the police, that they [were] doing everything they could to solve it."

In an effort to generate fresh tips, police put together a Crime Stoppers video in 2008 that depicts a re-enactment of the crime. Corporal Rick Jane with the RCMP historical homicide unit has since taken over as the primary investigator. He can't say much about the case, but he believes it can still be solved.

"I believe that all unsolved homicides can be solved," said Rick, who would not comment about any suspects or persons of interest. "We never give up hope that new information or evidence will be discovered that will allow the file to be solved."

Marie's untimely death is still painful for the remaining members of the Goudreau family. Daniel's father has since passed away, never knowing who murdered his little girl, but his eighty-nine-year-old mother is in good health following a stroke.

Marie was just graduating from high school when her life came to a sudden end. She had aspired to be a social worker so she could help others. "She wanted to make a difference," Daniel said. "[But] her future was robbed."

"I experienced a wave of emotions," he added. "Lots of anger at the start, but you can't harbour that kind of thing forever. You just have to let it go and move on with your life."

With every year that goes by, Daniel is less hopeful Marie's killer will ever be found.

With a flashlight in hand and the sun yet to rise, Constable Doug Green and his police dog, Ricco, made their way into a soggy Mill Woods ravine, following the track of a killer. At times the water was up to the officer's waist, but as the pair then climbed to the top of a hill littered with bushes, Doug found exactly what he was looking for—two sets of clear footprints in a muddy field, confirming the pair were on the right path.

Halfway through the field, Ricco stopped and stuck his head into the deep mud. Green thought the dog was distracted, but Ricco pulled out a white running shoe. The discovery was immediately reported over the police radio.

"Once I got the shoe, it was critical because I knew that one of the guys [suspects] would be missing a shoe. That was the biggest piece of the puzzle because that really was the smoking gun," said Doug, who had been with the Edmonton Police canine unit for four years when he got the call to respond to a Mill Woods home at 3455 42nd Street in April 1994.

At a pool hall the previous day, three teenagers had hatched a plan for a break and enter to get CDs. Without further discussion of their scheme, the trio left together and headed for Grant MacEwan College, where they pulled out a Safeway bag from behind a dumpster. Inside the bag was a stash of weapons. One teen grabbed a broken pool cue, while the others grabbed two knives wrapped in newspapers. They were all set for their crime.

After hanging out at a friend's house for a few hours in the Capilano neighbourhood, the trio chose Mill Woods for the burglary because it was known as a rich area. They were dropped off in the district at around 2 a.m. by an acquaintance and wandered aimlessly past many homes before picking one without cars in front, lights on, or security signs.

Slipping in through a basement window, the trio crept into the Danelesko family's dark basement and then into a hallway without stealing a thing. The youngest crook slipped into a bedroom and was preparing to rifle the dresser for cash, CDs, and jewelry when he heard a female's sleepy voice.

Barb Danelesko and her husband, Justin, were awoken around 4 a.m. by the sound of an off-the-hook phone beeping. She gently touched her husband to signal that he should stay in bed while she checked out the noise in the middle of the night. Thinking one of her two young sons might be up, Barb called out to both of them. Scott, then nine, answered. She called once more to five-year-old Todd as she left her room.

Barb reached for the light switch in the upstairs hallway outside her bedroom, but her hand instead encountered an intruder. Almost immediately a knife was thrust once into the base of the thirty-six-year-old's neck. The knife blade left a single, gaping 7.5-centimetre stab wound over the left breast, penetrating the heart.

"She never really screamed. All she did was sound totally surprised. 'Oh!' was all that she said in a high shriek. Then she did it again," said Justin, who got out of bed, thinking Barb had bumped into Todd.

"She ran back to the bed," he said of his wife, who he hadn't realized was clutching her chest. "There was no indication she was hurt."

Unaware of his wife's injury, Justin ran out of the bedroom and confronted two figures in the hallway. He grabbed and swung at them until they fled the home. As he turned to head back to the bedroom, he saw a third burglar, armed with two clubs.

"I told him to get the fuck out of here," Justin said. "I unlocked the door and opened it. He walked right by me and ran out the door."

Hearing Scott's screams, Justin rushed back to the bedroom and saw Barb slumped over the bed unconscious. Scott phoned 911 while Justin applied CPR in a desperate bid to revive his unconscious wife. Paramedics rushed Barb to the University Hospital, where she died from her injury.

By the time Doug and Ricco arrived at the Danelesko household, it was a chaotic scene full of emergency personnel. The pair headed up the street from the house and came across a pool cue and an iron bar that had been dropped as the suspects fled. From there, Doug and Ricco crossed a school field into the soggy ravine that eventually led them to the shoe. After finding the shoe, the pair followed the track into the Burnwood neighbourhood. That's when Green received a call from a duty officer, who was driving through Capilano and spotted two teens running north. Both were wearing their pants inside out and had one black shoe each, immediately painting them as possible suspects.

Doug was picked up and driven to where the teens had now been placed under arrest. The white runner found in the mud was placed on one of the suspect's bare feet. It was a perfect fit.

"I was pretty satisfied at that point because of the missing shoe and the time of the morning and the fact they were covered in mud," said Doug. "All the pieces were starting to fit together."

Doug returned to the field where the dog had found the shoe, hoping to find the second one. Ricco went deep into the footprint again, this time coming up with what Doug thought was a stick. Doug grabbed it from Ricco, cutting himself in the process. The stick was a knife.

"We had a shoe, a knife, and two clubs and that turned out to be some pretty significant evidence," Doug said, noting that two days later another knife was found in a neighbour's backyard near the Danelesko home. "You can't express how difficult that situation is for the family, the neighbourhood. From a police perspective, these are the kinds of files you want to solve."

Within two hours of the cold-blooded murder, two of the suspects had been picked up and cuffed. The hunt was on for the third suspect, who was found less than a week later at an apartment suite at 10730 104th Street. The teen had eluded police partly because officers were unable to get his identity from the other two suspects.

The random attack against a well-liked family rocked the city and left an entire community in mourning. All of the neighbourhood kids played at the Danelesko home, and neighbours knew Barb as a friend.

She had grown up in the town of Westlock, sixty-five kilometres northwest of the city, but had become a pillar of Mill Woods, teaching swimming lessons, volunteering on several parent committees at Minchau school, and coaching figure skating. She took kids in after school and knew many more through her own sons and volunteer activities.

Barb's death brought tears and outrage to the quiet neighbourhood and prompted an outcry from the public and victims' rights groups, who demanded harsher sentences for young offenders. Many residents were left feeling powerless and vulnerable in their own homes, wondering whether it could have happened to them. Some frightened neighbours began to barricade their property.

"This is like Mister Rogers' neighbourhood. We never thought in a million years this would happen," said Bill Mosier, who lives a couple of doors down from the Daneleskos. "My wife wants to buy a gun. I keep a baseball bat handy."

Barb Gagnon didn't know how to comfort her seven-year-old son when she found him crying in bed one night. He was overwhelmed by the darkness, being in bed and having to go to sleep—circumstances that reminded him of his friend Barb Danelesko's death.

"He was in bed crying and crying and he said, 'If that should happen to you, I'll crawl under the bed for the rest of my life,'" said Gagnon.

In the months following the loss of their beloved mother, Todd and Scott struggled with fears resulting from the crime. Too frightened to sleep alone, the boys shared a bed. Todd also slept with a white teddy bear. Both were afraid of the dark. When the nightmares came, the pair would dash across the hallway—lit with a night light—and crawl under the covers for the safety of their dad. For Christmas that year, all they wished for was justice to punish those who left them without a mother.

"I think those robbers should stay in jail forever," said Todd. His brother echoed the sentiment.

Barb and Justin met in the mid-1970s, when she was a commerce student at the University of Alberta. It was Barb's smile that caught Justin's attention, making it easy for him to talk to her. It was as if he'd known her his entire life. Nearly fifteen years after their wedding, Justin remained deeply in love with his wife. So secure was their love for each other, Barb used to jokingly point out attractive women to him.

On their seventh wedding anniversary, Justin rented a billboard and plastered it with a message signed by him and Scott. They put it up on 50th Street so Barb would see it on her way to work. The couple shared a belief that nothing was more important than the happiness of their family, and Barb drew strength and happiness from things she did for others.

"She was someone whose first thought was always of her family. She was very well loved. She had no enemies. I can't think of anyone who disliked her," said Justin, who was riddled with guilt following Barb's death, angry with himself that she walked into the scene alone.

"Do you have any idea what it's like to lose your life?" Justin asked rhetorically. "I don't mean physically, as in a car accident, but lost your life. If there were anything in the world I could possibly do to get her back..."

One teenager, who can't be named because he was tried and sentenced in youth court, was later convicted of manslaughter and given a three-year sentence for his role in the slaying—the maximum sentence for a young offender. More than three years after Barb was fatally stabbed, the two other teens, Sonny Head, who was sixteen at the time of the murder, and Dave Larocque, who had been fifteen, stood in a courtroom, where they were tried as adults, and admitted to the killing.

"Guilty," said a pony-tailed Sonny Head after the court clerk asked him how he pleaded to second-degree murder. The unexpected guilty pleas from Head, now nineteen, and co-accused Larocque, now eighteen, brought a dramatic and unexpected end to the court proceedings.

After their arrest, the pair were transferred to adult court but fought the move all the way to the Supreme Court, a battle they ultimately lost. Larocque pleaded guilty to manslaughter. All indications were that Head had inflicted the fatal wound. He was sentenced to life in prison with no chance of parole for seven years.

Flanked by friends and family, Head spoke to the parole board in June 2002 at the Stan Daniels Healing Centre in Edmonton. His new wife told the board that Head had changed. He was working, becoming more responsible, taking part in cultural events, and had increased contact with family and friends.

Head told the board he never intended to kill Barb, but he panicked and lashed out because he was scared. Guilt over the murder torments him, he said, adding that his biggest fear is that some day he will run into his victim's family.

"No matter what I do or what I say nothing's going to bring her back," said the then twenty-four-year-old convicted killer. "It was senseless how much pain I caused."

By this time, Head was already leaving the healing centre on unescorted temporary absences to work in a city shop. News that the man who killed their loved one was now walking the streets was upsetting to the Danelesko family.

"What about my wife's right to live?" asked Justin. "What happened to her rights? What about my sons' rights, to go to sleep at night in their house and feel safe?"

Members of the parole board noted that Head had combined traditional Aboriginal and mainstream programs to control his anger and substance abuse problems. He had also been a model prisoner, resisting the pressure to join prison gangs.

Eight years after Barb's senseless death, Head was granted day parole.

"It's frightening. I'm worried for the whole neighbourhood, and I don't think he's ready to go out," said Barb's mother, Kay, who went to counseling with her family to help deal with her grief. "I'll never get over it. It was a brutal, senseless thing," she said.

Head's time as a free man didn't last long. His parole was temporarily suspended and he was sent to the Drumheller Institution after a public argument with his wife over a Denny's coupon in which he threatened violence. During another hearing before the parole board in October 2003, Head said he hoped to lead an honest and respectful life as a way to honour his victim. When asked how he would do so, the now twenty-five-year-old started to cry. Head was again granted full parole. His release and statements further outraged Kay.

"I know his sob story. It doesn't mean anything, any of it. He's conning the system. He knows how to work the system, what to do and what to say," she said.

Five years later, Head lost his parole again for repeatedly drinking in violation of his release conditions. This time, parole board members didn't give him another chance and revoked Head's parole to keep him locked up at the Pê Sâkâstêw minimum-security facility in Hobbema, south of Edmonton. The board's decision meant Head had lost his freedom for at least another year. Kay hoped his return to jail would prod him to deal with his problems, something she thought should have already happened.

"By now, with all the treatments, he should have smartened up," she said.

MISSING PERSONS AND THE CASE OF LYLE AND MARIE MCCANN

Every time Bret McCann walks into his parents' home in St. Albert, he's hit with a flood of memories and a wave of emotions. It's the home where he spent much of his childhood, and not much has changed. Family pictures still hang on the wall, his father's books rest by his favourite chair, and the house is perfectly clean, just like his mother always kept it. The only thing missing is his parents.

"When I go in there, it smells like my mom still lives there. It makes me a little uncomfortable. All the memories come flooding back. It's difficult," says Bret.

The last time anyone saw Lyle McCann, seventy-eight at the time, and his seventy-eight-year-old wife, Marie, was in St. Albert, just northwest of Edmonton, on July 3, 2010. Driving a Sunvoyager RV towing a Hyundai Tucson, the seniors were fuelling up at a gas station, about to make their way to Chilliwack, B.C., for a vacation. They were scheduled to meet their daughter in nearby Abbotsford, but the couple never arrived. Two days later, their RV was found engulfed in flames near the Minnow Lake campground, twenty kilometres southeast of the town of Edson, Alberta. Six days later, the SUV they were towing was discovered in a remote wooded area near Carrot Creek, thirty kilometres east of Edson. Despite exhaustive efforts to find the missing couple, their bodies have yet to be recovered.

Not a day goes by when Bret doesn't think about his parents and what might have happened to them. The nightmare begins as soon as he wakes up. He can't get away from it. His heart is always heavy.

Family gatherings have become exceptionally difficult. A year after his parents disappeared, Bret's daughter celebrated the birth of a baby girl—the McCann's second grandchild. The daughter was especially close to Bret's parents. At the baby shower, everyone was well aware that someone was missing.

"My mom would have just been in her element with that [the baby shower]," said Bret. "We really missed my mom not being there, so that was very painful."

Not long after the couple disappeared, for reasons not disclosed by police, a career criminal named Travis Vader was charged with first-degree murder in their deaths. But the charges were stayed about a month before the trial, only to be brought back in December 2014. As of this writing, the case is before the courts.

A $60,000 reward remains posted for information leading to the whereabouts of the McCanns, and the family maintains a website for tips and information about the case, which was also posted on the Alberta Missing Persons and Unidentified Human Remains website.

Alberta police agencies and the chief medical examiner launched the site in 2008 as an additional tool to help detectives move investigations forward. It was closed down in 2014, when its content was moved to the national website (www.canadasmissing.ca) to give the cases more exposure. While it was up, though, the site contained the names of up to 196 people who were last seen at a certain date and location. A list and details of sixteen cases of unidentified human remains were posted on the site as well. Those listed had been missing for more than six months or went missing due to suspected foul play or mental-health issues. Cases were added when investigating agencies needed help and submitted information.

"It's important to be aware that not all people reported missing by their families are actually missing," said Corporal Lea Turner with the RCMP serious crimes branch. "Some have left on their own volition, and in some cases the person was found and refused to return to his or her family."

Some missing persons cases are believed to be homicides, but in most cases investigators don't have enough information to determine the possible cause of a person's

Bret McCann, son of Lyle and Marie McCann, poses next to a billboard advertising a reward for information about the missing couple on Highway 16 west of Edmonton. (Photo by Codie McLachlan / Courtesy of Sun Media)

disappearance. Some missing persons lived a high-risk or vulnerable lifestyle, having been involved with a gang, the drug trade, or the sex trade, while others were simply hitchhiking. In those cases, Lea said foul play could be considered a factor in their disappearance. Other people have gone missing in boating accidents, while mountain climbing, or have become lost while hunting in the woods. Some have wandered from care facilities. Regardless of the circumstances of how they disappeared, many have left a gaping hole in the lives of their loved ones.

"Sometimes [people] give up hope that they will be found alive and are hoping that the person's remains will be found so they can have closure," said Lea. "Others never give up hope."

Bret McCann is one of those people who has never given up hope. He knows the family must move forward as much as possible and has come to accept that his parents are gone. His dad won't be coming home to finish reading his book or to cut the lawn. The family photos have now come down off the walls, and dealings with the estate have been finalized.

Bret has bought a headstone for the plot his father had purchased in St. Albert. But standing at the site only reminds him that the final resting place of his parents is still not known. His voice fills with sadness as he talks about the emotional journey he's been on since 2010. As he continues to live and work in the city he grew up in, not a day goes by that Bret isn't reminded of his loving parents. Closure is now something he wants more than ever.

"I really didn't understand this closure thing for the longest time, but as the years go by, I think I do," said Bret. "To me, it's like they just went away. I think knowing what happened to them, knowing where their remains are, being able to bury their remains is important. It's important to give them a rest where my dad bought this plot and where he planned to be buried with my mother."

One of the things Bret cherishes the most is a family portrait of his parents, brother, and children taken by a professional photographer in the late 1980s at a St. Albert park. The photograph now hangs in his living room. Every time he looks at it, Bret can't help but think, *how sad*.

"Almost every day before I go to bed I have a look at that picture," he said, adding that his daughter's child is now two years old, and there's another baby on the way.

"My mother would have loved to have been part of that."

John Strikwerda knew something was terribly wrong the moment he saw that the curtains were closed at the north Edmonton home his brother-in-law lived in. In October 2007, he was sent to the residence to check on Robert Brodyk after he had failed to phone his mother to tell her the number of trick-or-treaters he had received on Halloween. It was something the fifty-six-year-old did every year.

Robert's mother had tried calling her son numerous times the following morning, but there was no answer. Her concern grew when he didn't show up for work at the nearby Save-On-Foods grocery store at the Londonderry Mall. A co-worker from the store went to check on him at the house he rented at 14408 65th Street and discovered his truck was missing, but there was no sign of the reliable employee.

When John went to the residence with the landlord that evening, they weren't able to open the front door, as something appeared to be blocking it. The pair entered the home through the back door and found Robert lying on the floor in the front entrance. He had been bludgeoned to death with a baseball bat, later found in a dark corner of the basement. The discovery was heartbreaking.

"It was totally devastating. When we couldn't open the front door, I just knew something had happened. Even when we drove up. He always had his front curtains wide open. They were pulled tight shut. That was the first indication something was amiss," said John. "A guy is in his own house and he gets bludgeoned to death. What kind of an animal can do this sort of thing?"

Robert was last seen alive at around 5:30 p.m. on Halloween night by neighbours who saw him through his dining-room window. Two days later, his missing pickup truck—a rusty two-tone 1987 Ford F-150 Lariat with a matching light blue canopy—was found parked in a lot behind a Co-op gas bar at 82nd Street and 127th Avenue. Police staked out the truck and asked neighbouring businesses if they had any security cameras monitoring the lot, but no leads resulted in the case. Officers believe the violent slaying could have been a break and enter that was interrupted. Detective Dave Morrissey, the lead investigator at the time, is still puzzled by the unsolved case.

Robert Brodyk's pickup truck, found November 2, 2007. (Photo courtesy of Sun Media)

"As far as we can determine right now, or at the time, there was no reason for this to happen at all," said Dave. "You can't determine any motives. Why was this fellow picked? Was it totally random? It appears that it was. You can't determine why it happened or have even any really solid idea as to what happened."

When Shirley Strikwerda received the news about her brother's death, she drove to her mother's house immediately.

"I needed to be with her. She was terrified," said Shirley. "Halloween is always a weird time of year. You see dark things. And then to have a murder take place in the family on Halloween night—it was horrible."

Shirley cherishes many fond memories of her brother, who remained friends with his ex-wife and close with his two daughters despite divorce. She remembers Robert as a family man who was a good dancer, joked around, and had a love for country music. Her husband, John, spent many hours shooting pool with Robert in his basement and worked closely with him on a cabin they had out of town.

"I miss dancing with my brother. I would dance with him at weddings and family functions. He would always make you laugh. He was a quiet fellow, but had a big heart. He would do anything for anybody," said Shirley, as she choked back tears.

Sometimes the memories are too painful for Shirley to recall. "You put this away in some little compartment in the back of your mind, and you don't deal with it. That's the way you carry on," Shirley said. "But there are many times when the memories come out, and they are very raw, and they take you back to that day immediately—like it happened yesterday."

The fact that somebody has gotten away with murder doesn't sit well with Robert's family, who've been through a roller coaster of emotions. John still harbours anger that somebody could be so violently killed in his own home. Robert's children miss their father terribly. Although several years have passed since Robert's murder, Shirley would like nothing more than to see the killer put behind bars.

"It's a mystery, and we feel that there is some unfinished business. It's not closed for us. We still can't believe that somebody has gotten away with this. We aren't sure if they are even around anymore," said Shirley, who has many unanswered questions.

"It's a senseless loss. My brother died for who knows what reason. It leaves us violated, too. It cost his life. Why? We don't know why. I would like the person who did this to pay for what they did."

John and Shirley have been in touch with police about the case from time to time, but they haven't received as much information as they were hoping for. With so much crime in the city stretching police resources thin, Shirley fears the case will continue to remain cold. John, however, knows police won't rest until they find the killer, but he has little faith that the justice system would sentence the culprit appropriately.

"It's almost at the point where I couldn't care less," he said. "I think the police department is doing due diligence. To what extent they have gone into this case, I don't know. The police would love to solve every crime, but to say that it's going to happen—probably not. I don't know if there will ever be closure. Bob's dead. You can't bring back the dead."

Wayne Kreutz had a long list of enemies. The forty-six-year-old businessman was known for arguing with customers at his used-car lot in north Edmonton and giving them bogus warranties. His behaviour on the lot perfectly matched the negative used-car salesman stereotype, and it may have cost him his life.

"The norm was to hate him," said Edmonton Police Superintendent Brad Doucette, who was once a detective on the case. He remembers it vividly. "There was nothing out of bounds for him. He was a bully, and if he didn't like you, he'd throw you right off the lot."

Moments after his business partner drove away on Halloween night in 1998, Wayne was shot in the chest outside his car lot at 15607 128A Avenue. The bullet entered the side of the three-hundred-pound man's chest and lodged in his heart. He was found clinging to life at the lot's gate at around 6:30 p.m. by a couple driving past to look at a car.

Robbery was not the motive, since Wayne still had a substantial amount of cash and jewelry on him. Detectives believe the shooter waited—maybe behind a hill across from the lot—until Wayne was alone before firing.

Wayne's wife, Donna, was on her way back to Edmonton after taking their youngest daughter to Spruce Grove to trick-or-treat with her cousins. She made nachos for supper, then phoned Wayne to see what time he would be home and if he could grab some coffee cream along the way. He said, "no problem," then the phone went dead. Donna tried calling back, but there was no answer. Thinking his battery had died, Donna took supper out of the oven and left it on the stove. Hours ticked by.

It wasn't unusual for Wayne to say he was coming home in fifteen minutes, then show up two hours later. Donna had been through this before, but this time she was getting angry.

"I was on the phone talking with one of my girlfriends that night and it was about quarter to nine. I said, 'Oh yeah, that's really nice of him,'" she said.

There was a knock at the door. Donna peered outside and saw a man standing on her doorstep. Given it was Halloween, she wasn't sure about letting him into her home, even after he identified himself as an Edmonton Police officer.

"He said, 'There's been an accident and it involves Wayne.' He said, 'He's been shot and he's deceased.' I said, 'Are you kidding me?'" said Donna, adding her husband of seventeen years was a practical joker.

"He said, 'No, this is legitimate.' I lost it at that point. I just couldn't believe it. I just hit the ground. My head was spinning. It was such a shock. I just could not believe it."

It was a homicide with too many suspects. Police questioned up to fifty people on Wayne's long list of enemies—including an outlaw biker-gang associate—and some were glad to see him dead. But the killer still remains on the loose, and the case has become a thorn in Brad Doucette's side.

"That was the frustrating part of the file. There were so many suspects, and we were never able to actually identify and charge someone," said Brad, who worked in the homicide unit for seven years. "In my experience, I've never run into a case that had so many people who had that sort of dislike for [someone]."

No matter how dodgy the father of two's business practice was, he still had people who loved him dearly. His sudden death began a nightmare for his family and is something Donna never expected would happen in a million years. In order to make ends meet, Donna took on two jobs, and she stayed strong for her daughters, only crying for her husband in private.

Donna was fourteen when she met Wayne at a car lot he worked at. She didn't like him at first and never thought that some day this man who was six years older than her would end up being her husband and the father of her two children. The car business was Wayne's life, along with his family. It wasn't a fairy-tale marriage, but the girls always had everything they needed. The couple's youngest daughter was only twelve years old at the time of his death and has never gotten over the loss.

"She was just devastated. She was extremely close to her dad," Donna said. "When she talks about her dad she still to this day bawls her face off. It does not go away."

Wayne's twenty-three-year-old daughter Leanne became pregnant with her second child a year after the shooting. Her father loved her then-twenty-month-old daughter and would have been overjoyed with the prospect of becoming a grandfather of two.

"My daughter was just the world to him and now he won't be around to share in this," said Leanne, choking back tears. "He did make some people mad, but if you knew my dad, you'd know he was a good person. His bark was worse than his bite. If he did hurt anybody, it was just with words. I want to know who did this and why they took my dad away."

Brad continued to speak with Wayne's mother every couple of months until she passed away. The youngest of five children, Wayne was the apple of his mother's eye. His murder left her devastated, just like the rest of his family.

At his funeral, friends remembered Wayne as a great guy who treated his loved ones like gold. He doted on his daughter, recalled Brad, and they were very tight, but if Wayne didn't like you, he could make your life miserable.

Brad believes the shooting was planned, given the timing and the secluded location on a dead-end road. The detective is confident he's spoken with the man who pulled the trigger, but that man has kept tight-lipped about the evil he's done, and a lack of evidence has prevented the case from moving forward. With the right information, however, Brad believes the case can easily be solved.

Wayne Kreutz. He was forty-six years old when he was shot and killed outside his used-car lot on October 31, 1998. (Photo courtesy of Sun Media)

"We planted some seeds with him [the killer] back then, but barring new information—like him growing a conscience—it's going to be very difficult. I think this is one of those things where the guy who did it didn't tell a soul. At some point either he'll tell someone or maybe he'll come clean on his death bed," said Brad. "There's one dead guy, but there's a lot of victims and that damage and pain and wound often never heals. You are doing it for the victim's families. You want to give them closure."

Donna hates Halloween. It's a night she calls depressing, along with Christmas Eve—the night she and Wayne were married in 1981. Wayne's birthday is about a month later. Donna still lights a white candle on the date every year in his memory.

It's been a long time since Donna has heard anything from police about the investigation. But even though seventeen years have passed, she remains hopeful the case will be solved.

"It's still there. You still think about it and you still wonder. I would still love to know not only who, but why," she said. "It's very devastating. It ruined all our lives, but I hold out hope that one day I will see that person face to face. The anger I have is unbelievable. It's like hatred. My daughter has a lot of emotional issues because of that, and that will never ever be taken away or made better. Time heals, but only to a certain point."

SANGEETA KHANNA

S angeeta Khanna's future looked bright. Following a bitter divorce in 2002, the forty-one-year-old mother purchased a new house in south Edmonton where she lived with her only son. Having worked in a clerical job with Alberta Permit Pro for a year, Sangeeta was ecstatic about landing a lucrative $3 million contract with a major energy company for her firm. It would have doubled her salary.

Sangeeta had close ties to her large, tight-knit family, so there was no reason for her to up and leave. When she disappeared on April 17, 2006, those who knew her suspected something was wrong.

"There's no way she would take off," said Sangeeta's older sister, Krishna Mohan. "She's very responsible. I know her so well."

Sangeeta left her Ellerslie Crossing home earlier that night to do some banking at the Mill Woods Town Centre before picking up some ice cream. When her dad called her cell phone at around 9 p.m., she told him she was just leaving her house to drive to the bank. Two hours later, Sangeeta called her fifteen-year-old son, Kuran, at home. She told him to go to bed and that she would be home in five minutes, but Kuran sensed from the nervous tone in his mother's voice that something was wrong. He decided to wait up, but she didn't come home. As the hours ticked by, the teen eventually fell asleep at his computer desk. When he woke up later that morning, he was alarmed to find his mother still hadn't returned.

Scared and worried, Kuran went to school and told a friend what had happened. His friend's mom called the police, who later found Sangeeta's abandoned blue 2005 Suzuki Grand Vitara in the parking lot of the Royal Bank near 23rd Avenue and 66th Street in Mill Woods. Two plastic food containers sat on the passenger seat on top of a plastic bag. In the back seat were two pairs of running shoes, a shoebox, a folded cadet uniform, and a skateboard, among other mundane, everyday items. There were no signs of a struggle or foul play in or around the vehicle. No activity had been recorded on her bank account that night, either. Police don't believe she ever made it into the building.

Former Edmonton Police Homicide Detective Ernie Schreiber was the primary investigator on the case. Based on information passed on by the officers first at the scene, he immediately suspected foul play.

A past boyfriend of Sangeeta's set off alarm bells among the officers when he was questioned about what he had done the night of her disappearance. He claimed he was at a casino, then later came home and slept downstairs, but the man's wife told police that he was lying: he never came home that night.

"She [the man's wife] later told me directly, 'I will never lie for him [and] I'm also not going to cover for him,'" said Ernie, who called the man by the pseudonym "Anthony," since his name has never been released. The pair had a rocky relationship, said Ernie, only staying together so the family wouldn't fall apart.

Detectives looked inside Anthony's white Dodge Caravan and noticed that it had been meticulously cleaned recently, furthering their suspicions. But Anthony owned a cleaning business, so it was possible that his car was usually neat. He met Sangeeta through that cleaning business, which had been successful at one time, employing close to a hundred employees. As time went by, however, Anthony's gambling addiction got the best of him, causing his business to suffer.

Anthony and Sangeeta were romantically involved for about a year before she broke it off. Police convinced Anthony to voluntarily come in for questioning two days after Sangeeta went missing.

"He was very cooperative, said 'I'm here to help, I'm concerned.' When we dealt with him, he was very calm. When we left him alone in the interview room, he was pacing," said Ernie, adding that Anthony denied any involvement in Sangeeta's disappearance but acknowledged he had seen her recently.

Anthony gave police a rundown of what he had done on the night in question, but little things weren't adding up, such as when video surveillance was checked from businesses Anthony claimed he had been at: there was no sign of him. Still, he seemed to have an explanation for everything.

"He was a good liar and a chronic liar," Ernie said.

In the days following Sangeeta's bizarre disappearance, friends and family fanned out across the city to search for clues, focusing on areas such as hospitals and clinics. As the days turned into months with no sign of their Sangeeta, it became more and more difficult to stay positive.

"The whole family is shaky today. Everybody is down," said Sangeeta's other sister, Madhu Mohan, a few weeks after her disappearance. "We are hoping she comes home alive, but as the days are passing, it's getting scary."

It wasn't until April 2008 that police confirmed Sangeeta's family's suspicions that she was likely the victim of a homicide. A person of interest was now a suspect—information that came as news to the family.

When police seized Anthony's van earlier in the investigation, they had gone through it with a fine-tooth comb, tearing up the seats in the process. They found water underneath the mats in the rear of the van, and the carpet was soaked. Forensic investigators also discovered a tiny amount of blood on the side of the carpeted area. It was enough to obtain a DNA sample that showed it belonged to Sangeeta, but Anthony offered Ernie an explanation. Detectives also pulled surveillance video from a Safeway gas bar near the area in which Sangeeta disappeared. The video captured her pulling up and coming to a stop at around 11 p.m. Moments later, another vehicle—a white van the exact same model as Anthony's—pulled up beside her. The lights on Sangeeta's vehicle flashed, consistent with them being automatically locked, and then a shadow of her movement shows her getting into the van, which then pulls away. A key piece of the picture is missing, however—who's driving the van?

"We had the front headlights, but we didn't have anything above it. We couldn't see who it was," said Ernie, who firmly believes the other vehicle belonged to Anthony. "You play with the cards that you are dealt," he added. "We had an awful lot of good things happening."

Police looked at cell phone records to try and determine what happened next. Anthony's cell phone was turned off around the time he's believed to have met Sangeeta and wasn't turned back on until around 3 a.m. That's when the phone was traced near Meadow Lake, Saskatchewan—at least a four-hour drive from Edmonton. Anthony's wife said he had no connection to the area. Phone records also show Sangeeta had earlier received a call from a payphone at a Canadian Tire on 50th Street, not far from Anthony's cleaning business.

Even though they were unable to officially place Anthony under arrest, Ernie and his partner desperately tried to convince Anthony to come back to police headquarters for an interview. He was under surveillance, with detectives popping into the casino once in a while to see if he would talk, but Anthony hid behind the apron of his lawyer.

Anthony allowed police to go into his cleaning business and have a look around. Looking back, Ernie thinks detectives should have gone through it in more detail while they had the chance.

"We didn't go through it with a fine-tooth comb. It was an absolute sty. There was crap everywhere. He lived in there, slept in there at times," said Ernie. "There is a delicate balance. If we started to get too crazy with him at his business, he could shut us down. He was not a happy camper with us when we took his van."

Detectives tried several tactics on Anthony, including the use of undercover officers, but he was a loner with a gambling addiction, and didn't take the bait. Thinking he had more than enough evidence, Ernie approached the Crown prosecutor about laying charges. Without a body, however, he was told it would be difficult to prove there was, in fact, a murder.

"If it would have been up to me, I would have [laid charges]" said Ernie, adding the defence could have floated a theory she was left out there, not killed.

"When you add it [the Safeway gas bar video footage] into everything else, plus his provable lies, that's when you start saying there's fire, never mind smoke. But the problem is the legal hurdle of not having her body or the remains. We were prepared to say, *run it anyway*. There are some cases you just got to say, *damn the torpedo*."

Eventually Anthony moved to Kelowna, where the rest of his family lived. On one occasion, he ended up in the hospital due to heart problems, so Ernie and his partner paid him a visit at his bedside. Anthony's heart monitor went up the moment the two detectives flipped open the curtain, but he still wasn't willing to talk.

Years later, Anthony passed away from a heart attack, leaving many questions unanswered. Ernie finds it highly unlikely somebody else out there knows what happened on the night Sangeeta disappeared forever.

"He's taken his secret to the grave. There's not always happy endings. That's the tragic part of it. At the end of the day, he's gone. They may find the remains, and then it is no longer a missing person, but it may also never be a homicide investigation when he's the main suspect," said Ernie, who describes Sangeeta's family as incredibly wonderful people.

"As a homicide detective, there are cases where you just want so much to solve the case for the family. They were that family, and unfortunately I couldn't come through for them. In the end, you can't let that eat you up. You do your best and learn to deal with the outcome."

Sangeeta came to Canada from India in 1983. Her brother-in-law, Romesh Mohan, remembers her as a vibrant and good person. The family has moved on with their lives, trying to remember Sangeeta in a good way rather than dwelling on the past, but the pain is always there. It never goes away.

"It's painful to think about. We miss her every day," said Romesh. "We still love her. That's how families are. We have her memory in the form of her son, who is around us most of the time." Every time Romesh reads about remains being found or people going missing, a jolt ripples through his body.

"It [finding the remains] would bring closure definitely," Romesh added. "There is always hope."

All Johnny Altinger wanted was to find a companion. The thirty-eight-year-old lived a quiet life by himself, working at a machine shop in the community of Nisku, just south of Edmonton, as a quality-control inspector. He had a passion for race bikes, Transformers, and computer technology. Using a computer was one way Johnny met women.

On a Friday night in October 2008, Johnny was chatting online with a woman named Jen on the dating website, Plenty of Fish. She suggested that the pair meet and gave him directions to go to a garage in a back alley, then sneak in through a partially open door.

Before he left his home for the evening, Johnny was also chatting online with William Stanic and told him about the coming meeting with Jen. William thought the directions given by the woman were weird. Johnny also called his good friend Dale Smith, who smelled something fishy about the meeting and told Johnny to call him back with the address once he'd arrived.

Johnny called Dale back a short time later, saying the woman wasn't at the location provided. Instead he met a guy who was making a movie and had shown him a replica gun. Dale thought Johnny was going home for the night, but he later received an e-mail saying the meeting was on.

"She's home now. I'm heading over again! HEHE!" the e-mail read.

Three days later, an unusual e-mail was sent from Johnny's account to his friends and colleagues. In it, he told his supervisor that he quit his job and was going on an extended leave—a move that was highly uncharacteristic for a man who liked to plan. Johnny's friends received one message stating he had gone on a "nice long tropical vacation" to Costa Rica with an "extraordinary" woman. The e-mail did not contain any of Johnny's typical jokes and had his name at the end—something he never added.

Dale grew suspicious since Johnny didn't like hot places. Another friend, Debra Teichroeb, also had a hunch something was wrong. She noticed that the wording in a message she received wasn't in Johnny's usual style. He often called her "Sunshine," but he didn't this time around. A pit began to form in the bottom of her stomach.

"I thought they [the e-mail messages] were odd, to be honest," she said. "The John I knew did not do things on a whim. I found that strange."

Concerned about his well-being, several of Johnny's friends went to his south-side condo. Inside, they found Johnny's passport, toiletries, and beachwear, but his laptop was missing.

One of the friends, Carrie-Lynn Souza, sent an e-mail back to Johnny, asking him to contact Dale since everyone was concerned. She received a reply, saying there was no need to worry as he was "on vacation and loving it." The e-mail further stated he would be in touch with Dale soon and that he was "having the time of [his] life."

Johnny was having anything but the time of his life. He was no longer alive. Instead of meeting a woman named Jen at the address he was given, Johnny was bludgeoned over the head with a copper pipe, then stabbed with a hunting knife. The crazed killer proceeded to dismember his body and dump the remains down a city sewer. The remains were found months later.

Several days before Johnny disappeared, Gilles Tetreault was chatting with an attractive blonde named Sheena on Plenty of Fish when he was lured to the same garage, only to be confronted by a man wearing a hockey mask and holding a stun gun.

Gilles grabbed the stun gun, moved it to the side, and made a bolt for the door, but his attacker caught him, pulled a handgun, and ordered him to the floor with his head down and hands behind his back.

The thirty-six-year-old began to fear the worst when his eyes were covered with duct tape and he thought he heard his attacker unzip his pants. Thinking he might be raped, possibly killed, Gilles decided to fight back.

"I figured I would rather die my way than his," he said.

Gilles tore off the tape and turned to his attacker, who again pulled out the gun. Gilles grabbed it, realizing the weapon was actually plastic. A struggle ensued, but Gilles broke free, sliding underneath the garage door. He tried to run, but he fell down. The man with the hockey mask came out and dragged Gilles back inside.

For some reason the attacker briefly let go, allowing Gilles to get up and start running. He stumbled in front of a couple walking their dog and asked for help. The stunned couple instead walked away when a man wearing a hockey mask and hoodie pulled tightly around his face came outside.

An exhausted and hurting Gilles managed to get into his truck and speed away as the attacker retreated back to the garage. He later called police after hearing about

Johnny's disappearance, which detectives began investigating on October 17.

Two weeks later, a local filmmaker by the name of Mark Twitchell was arrested and charged with first-degree murder, beginning one of the most publicized murder cases in the city's history.

Using a government grant, Twitchell had been renting the Mill Woods garage to film his latest mystery-thriller, *House of Cards*, which he finished in late September. The film centres on a character who lures people into a garage, ties them to a chair and chops them into pieces. Neighbours sometimes heard the sound of chainsaws coming from the garage, which was situated behind a derelict home at 5712 40th Avenue.

In late August, Twitchell put out a casting call for actors to star in the film. He was looking for someone to play a killer who could deliver a cold, sociopathic tone. He also wanted to fill the role of the victim, portrayed as a family man laced with insecurity.

News of Twitchell's arrest sent a jolt throughout the city's film industry. The twenty-nine-year-old was a married man who lived in St. Albert with his wife and eight-month-old daughter. Friends had a hard time believing the locally respected filmmaker had turned his latest thriller into a murder. Some maintained he was innocent and hardly capable of committing such a vicious crime.

"Mark Twitchell is a good man who's been caught up in an unfortunate series of coincidences," said Mike Young, a long-time friend. "The most unfortunate of which is that the baseless police speculation makes for a really good news story. When he is acquitted, I hope the media sees fit to run his acquittal on the front page, just as big as they're running the stories now."

When questioned by police about Johnny's disappearance, Twitchell initially denied having any knowledge of it. But officers eventually got search warrants for the home of Twitchell's parents, his own home, car, and the rented garage, where they came upon a gold mine of evidence. Police spent days collecting what they found.

From the garage, investigators seized a hunter's game-processing kit, which included a butcher knife, a skinner knife, a boning/filleting knife, shears, a saw, meat cleaver, a carving fork, and rib spreaders—the only item that didn't have suspected blood on it. Inside a 45-gallon metal drum with a scorched area on the bottom was a possible tooth fragment, a gold ring, an arm from a pair of eyeglasses, and part of a zipper. The mounting evidence didn't end there.

Police also found a pair of handcuffs, an 800,000-volt stun baton, a BB handgun, and two threaded metal pipes, one of which was wrapped in blood-soaked fabric tape at one end. Both pipes appeared to have blood and a burned or charred substance on them. Large parts of the floor glowed blue when investigators used a chemical solution that reacts to the presence of blood. A large metal table also had blood on it, and a tooth fragment sat underneath. Testing later confirmed Johnny's DNA was in all of the blood.

A search of Twitchell's car provided more clues for detectives. Inside were several Post-it notes with hand-drawn directions leading from Twitchell's home to the south Edmonton condo where Johnny lived. Other notes had bizarre written instructions on them that read "kill room clean sweep," "return to addy of vic," "ship phone while it is on," "destroy wallet contents," and "use Wi-Fi for email."

Also in the car, detectives found the keys and remote car door opener for Johnny's red Mazda 3, and a backpack containing a laptop computer. Two knives were found with blood on them, along with a duffle bag, a roll of black tape, and a plastic gas can. Testing later showed the knives also had Johnny's DNA on them. Several bloodstains were also found in the trunk of the car.

At the Twitchell residence were more handwritten diagrams, illustrating a table and two chairs with arrows pointing at them, saying "victim chair" and "killer chair." A hockey mask with the mouth area cut out and suspected blood on it was discovered, and bloodstains were also found in the washing machine.

Despite the mountain of evidence police had to charge Twitchell with the grisly crime, one key piece of the puzzle was still missing—Johnny's body was nowhere to be found.

In his first interview with detectives, Twitchell went on at length about his aspiring career as a filmmaker. He spoke passionately and laughed several times, but when the subject changed to Johnny, Twitchell became guarded.

Detective Mike Tabler told Twitchell about the missing man, stating Johnny told friends he was meeting a girl at the garage Twitchell was renting. But Twitchell maintained he didn't know anything about it or how an oil drum inside had been scorched.

The day after the hour-long interview, Twitchell sent Mike an e-mail, stating there were a couple of odd things that were freaking him out that he wanted to share. Twitchell claimed he had been in his car parked near the Mill Woods garage when a man tapped on his window and offered to sell him a car—a red 2005 Mazda 3—the same kind as Johnny's. He said the guy told him he had hooked up with a really rich woman, so he was willing to take whatever cash Twitchell had for the vehicle. A deal was made for $40, and the car was driven to the nearby garage. Once there, Twitchell said the demeanour of the man changed, and the man suddenly needed to leave in a hurry. Twitchell also told Mike that his own car had been broken into days earlier at Southgate Mall, and several things were stolen.

"I can only imagine what the family of the missing guy must be going through," wrote Twitchell in the e-mail. "The whole thing is making me sick to my stomach."

On a following Sunday night, former Homicide Detective Bill Clark was getting ready to go home, when Twitchell came in out of the blue for another interview. The interview ran until 6 a.m. Bill didn't buy Twitchell's story from the get go.

"I knew the whole time he was telling me he was a liar, but I'm just sitting here smiling and letting him talk, letting him fill me up with all the lies," said Bill. "He really wasn't a good liar. Mark Twitchell's downfall was he had no idea how the police investigated anything. Despite all his reading, he really didn't check up on how we do things. He underestimated the police, and that worked out to our advantage."

In June 2009, when Twitchell was awaiting trial, detectives met him at the Edmonton Remand Centre, where he gave them a piece of folded paper that contained a Google map of north Edmonton with a hand-drawn red circle identifying a sewer in an alley. On the bottom was a handwritten note that said "Location of John Altinger's remains," along with detailed directions to a manhole. It was only a couple of blocks from the home of Twitchell's parents and half a block from where detectives stopped peering down manholes after several months of searching for Johnny. The detectives drove to the manhole later in the evening and peered inside. After months of searching, they had finally found what they were looking for.

"What I saw was what I believed to be two pieces of human remains within the sewer itself," said Detective Brad Mandrusiak, who decided to search the sewer the next morning in daylight.

About half of the bones typically seen in a human body were found in the sewer, mainly portions of the torso from the chin to the pelvis. Some of them had marks showing they had been cut with a sharp blade and sawed. Missing were the skull, limbs, and organs.

By now, the bizarre case was generating international attention. The U.S. network ABC was set to air a segment on the story on its current affairs show *20/20*. The appeal was the comparison to the television show *Dexter*, which portrays a fictional character who leads a double life as a cop and serial killer. Twitchell was an avid fan of the show, once posting a Facebook statement that he had "way too much in common with Dexter Morgan."

When the highly anticipated six-week trial began in March 2011, Twitchell pleaded not guilty to first-degree murder, but guilty of interfering with human remains. Crown prosecutor Lawrence Van Dyke rejected the plea, telling the jury Twitchell wanted to have the experience of killing another human being. Defence lawyer Charles Davison told the jury not all deaths are criminal and not all homicides are murder.

The most significant piece of evidence against Twitchell was buried in the laptop found in his car. In the computer's memory was a deleted document called "SKConfessions." Van Dyke believed the document was a diary written by the accused killer.

"This story is based on true events. The names and events were altered slightly to protect the guilty," read the opening lines of the thirty-some-page document, which details events mirroring what happened to both Gilles and Johnny. "This is the story of my progression into becoming a serial killer," it continues. "Like anyone just starting out in a new skill, I had a bit of trial and error in the beginning of my adventures. Allow me to start from the beginning and I think you'll see what I mean...."

The document goes on to explain the author's aspirations to kill using Internet dating sites to lure single men. It also details how the second victim arrived at the garage a few minutes early and caught the killer off guard, so he introduced himself as a filmmaker, showed the man a prop handgun, and told him the woman he was meeting was running late. The killer lured the same victim back to the garage using the dating site, saying the woman was now there. The writing also details how the killer went to the victim's home a few days later and authored an e-mail from the victim's account, advising that he was going on a two-month Caribbean vacation.

The writer goes on to recount a failed attempt at burning the victim's limbs and torso in a barrel in his parents' backyard. Abandoning that plan, he returns to the garage "kill room" to do more cutting so the body can be stuffed down a sewer. "It's an interesting feeling, driving around town with what used to be a human body bagged up in your trunk."

The author describes the time between the murder and disposing of the evidence, writing about his home life with his wife and young daughter, as well as his mistress. He speaks of spending a day trying to burn bags of human remains in a barrel in his parents' backyard, and then going home to his wife and child, who he plays with, feeds, and bathes before putting her to bed. The author chats online with his mistress, then heads out to the woman's home once his wife is asleep. The names of three characters in the document are nearly identical to the names of Twitchell's real wife, daughter, and girlfriend at the time.

The story ends with the author slicing open hefty bags containing the remains of the victim, and then dumping them into a manhole. The killer returns to the garage, burning all the evidence that he thinks is left. A key issue for the court was whether the document represented fact or fiction.

Twitchell's then ex-wife broke down several times during her testimony, speaking about the former couple's young daughter and the problems they were having with their marriage. The pair met in 2005 through an Internet dating site and married two years later, but it wasn't happily ever after. At the time of the murder, they were in marriage counselling and living separate lives. The last day Jess Twitchell saw her husband was on October 21, 2008, when police came to the couple's home.

"They thought Mark had killed someone, murdered him," she said, noting her husband said he was at the gym on the day of the murder. They were together the following day and went on a date. There was nothing unusual about Twitchell's mood or his appearance.

That same October, Twitchell had begun exchanging messages on Facebook with a fellow *Dexter* fan in Cleveland, Ohio. The conversation turned dark when the woman began talking about what she would like to do to her ex-husband's current wife. Twitchell gave the woman advice on murder and how to get away with it, suggesting a sturdy copper pipe would be more effective than a stun gun to apprehend a victim. He also discussed using a hunter's game-processing kit to cut up a body, but the woman said she would never be able to do that, adding "dark fantasies are...just a fantasy." A day after Johnny's slaying, Twitchell told the woman he crossed the line and liked it. The woman eventually sent the messages to Edmonton Police.

When it was Twitchell's time to take the stand, he admitted he was indeed the author of "SKConfessions," but told the jury that while some of it was true, some of it was also made up.

Twitchell tearfully admitted he killed and dismembered Johnny, but he said it was all in self-defence. When the thirty-one-year-old lured Johnny to the garage, he told him the date was a hoax and part of a multimedia-format psychological thriller he was producing. But Johnny became angry and the pair exchanged harsh words, ultimately sparking a fight.

According to Twitchell, Johnny grabbed a pipe lying against a wall and took a couple of swings. Twitchell snatched the pipe from Johnny's hands, hitting him several times on the head until an angry Johnny grabbed it back.

At that point, Twitchell said he pulled out a hunting knife that was in a sheath attached to his belt. When Johnny came swinging,

Johnny Altinger. The thirty-eight-year-old was lured to an Edmonton garage, where he was stabbed and dismembered by local filmmaker Mark Twitchell. (Photo courtesy of Sun Media)

Twitchell stabbed him, then froze for five to ten minutes as Johnny staggered backwards and fell to the floor.

"It happened so fast. I just remember a wet sensation on the hand holding the handle, and I just let go. Then I saw it sticking out of him," said Twitchell, who began crying as he admitted not doing anything to help Johnny. Instead of calling 911, he decided to dismember the man he had lured to his garage, putting the remains into garbage bags in the back of Johnny's car.

"I felt a lot weaker, like a piece of scum or a piece of shit," said Twitchell, when questioned about the parts of the document where the author describes himself as feeling stronger and above other people while dismembering the victim's body.

Like the homicide detectives investigating the case, the six men and six women on the jury didn't buy Twitchell's story and found him guilty after five hours of deliberations and weeks of testimony from some forty witnesses. Twitchell was sentenced to life in prison with no chance of parole for twenty-five years. The sentence brought some relief to Johnny's heartbroken family.

Johnny's brother, Gary, who travelled from B.C. for the trial, spoke of the ordeal. "Over the last several weeks, and of course over the last couple of years, our family has been exposed to such grief that no human being should ever feel," he said. Gary described his little brother as the most selfless person, a gentle and good friend to all, adding that losing his only sibling has taken a terrible toll, causing recurring nightmares of not being able to help Johnny in his time of need.

Johnny's mother, Elfriede, doesn't think there will ever be closure. Each day she's filled with a feeling of numbness, and she takes antidepressants just to endure the passage of time. Until the phone company reassigns her son's phone number, Elfriede calls just to hear him talk on the voice-mail greeting.

"He was a wonderful, kind, caring human being, but we will move on to the next step, I think, and start to heal, if that's possible," she said. "People have asked me if I wish there was still the death penalty, and I must answer no. My wish is for the perpetrator of this unforgivable and horrific act to reflect on his actions and die a slow death every day of his life."

VICTIMS OF HOMICIDE

Jane Orydzuk is not an angry person, but sixteen years ago she experienced that emotion on an unimaginable scale. Not a day goes by that Jane doesn't think about her thirty-three-year-old son, Tim Orydzuk, and October 1, 1994, the day he was murdered. Tim went to work that day at the CPL Paperboard plant in Sherwood Park, a community just east of Edmonton, to repair a baler that was broken. Instead, he met his death alongside his twenty-four-year-old friend, James Dieter. When their bodies were discovered, police originally thought the pair had been electrocuted, but thirty-six hours later, a medical examiner discovered three bullet holes in each man's skull.

Tim was a loving son, husband, uncle, grandson, brother, and father to a four-year-old girl born with a mop of black hair and oval eyes. Jane remembers that when Tim was a child he spent hours watching his dad building and fixing things. Eventually, Tim had his own family, and he had big dreams for a life in the country, but those dreams didn't even have a chance to bloom.

The months following Tim's death are a blur for Jane. She struggled every day to put one foot in front of the other. It wasn't until she caught her breath that reality set in. Then came the anger.

Jane's husband, Ted, never got over his anger or the anguish of losing his only son, and he died of a stroke on a cold and frosty Christmas Eve in 2004. Before Ted's death, Jane had often wondered if smiles would ever return to her husband's face, if there was any chance for happiness again. The only comfort Jane found on Christmas Day that year was knowing her husband and son were together again in a place that knows no pain.

Several months after Tim's death, Jane attended a Compassionate Friends meeting, where she met an Edmonton couple whose son had also been murdered. The trio quickly realized they didn't fit in with the rest of the group, mainly comprised of parents who had lost children to drunk drivers, suicides, or Sudden Infant Death Syndrome. The pain Jane and the couple were feeling was different, so they began their own meetings, thus founding the Victims of Homicide Support Society.

The trio met at the couple's Edmonton home for about seven years, until the group was forced to find a larger venue due to the number of people who had joined. Since Tim's death, Jane has found a strength she never knew she had, but in order to reach that point, she's had to endure emotional pain few people will ever encounter. Today she attributes much of her strength to the support she has received from the society.

"Nobody else gets it. It's a whole different journey when it's a homicide. It's such a traumatic thing compared to a normal death," said Jane. "People don't know what to do with you. They don't know what to do with your pain, so it gets to the point where they avoid you at all costs. You lose friends; it divides families."

When Jane formed the society, it didn't take long before she began to feel comfort in talking to those who've also had the lives of loved ones taken by the hands of another. During the meetings, members of the group talk about their anger at the justice system, defence lawyers, going to trials with hope and coming out totally defeated. On some nights, society members are joined by grief counselors; other times, they choose to remember all the fun things about their loved ones and the joy they brought to their lives. A few members are riddled with guilt, obsessing over an argument or dilemma they had with their loved ones prior to the deaths, and how things could have been different. The group now has about forty active members that meet once a month to find some healing. The bond members form is instant.

"It's a very lonely journey unless you can connect with other people who have walked that walk. People look at you as if you're supposed to be getting over this," said Jane, who now devotes her life to helping others get through their anger and pain. Everyone's journey is unique. Jane has been blown away by the healing she has witnessed.

"Many of us have moved on," she said. "But it's not something you ever find closure in. You go through some anger, and eventually it's a sink-or-swim thing. You have to move forward, but it's years before you feel that level in you and just let it go. You don't forget, you just have to move past it and get on with your life in positive ways."

A suspect was arrested and charged with the double murder twenty-two months after Tim and James were murdered. Five years after Tim's death, the matter finally went to trial, but the family didn't hold much hope for a conviction.

In September 1998, Jane's family was thrown into turmoil once again when Jason Dix, the man charged with killing James and Tim, walked from court a free man. In a dramatic turn of events just days before the trial was set to resume, the Crown dropped its first-degree murder case against Dix, on the grounds there was no reasonable likelihood of a conviction.

Tim's relatives were shocked as they watched Dix hug and shake hands with family and friends outside the courtroom.

"The justice system has failed us," said Tim's sister, Valerie, while another sister sobbed at her side.

"Two guys are dead. No one's been convicted. It's a travesty of justice," said Tim's brother-in-law, Tom Olsen.

Jane was at the court proceedings every day. It was something she felt she owed to her son. But as the days in the trial went on, the family started losing hope that the case would ever have the outcome they wanted. Jane said the trial became a power struggle between the defence and Crown.

"They were both high-profile lawyers," said Jane. "They had fought many years in the courtroom. After days, you would listen to them and say, this isn't even about Tim and James, it's about who's going to win the case. There is no justice for victims in the courts, absolutely none."

The case had been dogged by problems, including allegations of police and prosecutorial misconduct. The trial began in April 1997, but it ground to a halt after fifteen days, when a senior prosecutor withdrew amid complaints about his conduct. Another prosecutor later said the withdrawal played no part in the decision to dismiss the charges.

When the case was dismissed, Dix had spent almost two years in jail since his arrest at his workplace in July 1996. He told reporters outside the courthouse he was "overjoyed and relieved" by the decision, maintaining his innocence.

"I had absolutely nothing to do with this," he said, adding, "I hope the police will find the person or people responsible for this crime."

After the court proceedings, Dix's lawyer said the case was so weak it should never have gone to trial. He also added there was a possibility of civil action. A year later, Dix acted on what his lawyer said and sued the Crown and RCMP, eventually receiving $765,000 for his troubles.

Although much time has passed since Tim's untimely death, Jane's memory of her only son is still very strong. His soft, deep voice saying "Aw, c'mon mom" is permanently etched in her mind. And although Jane has managed to find inner peace, she's no longer optimistic that Tim's killer will ever be brought to justice. Even if something did surface now, she wouldn't want to go through it all over again.

"People say, 'Wouldn't it be wonderful if you heard some news?'" Jane said. But she disagrees. "I don't want to go back there. We sat in courtrooms for four years, and I don't want to do that now that my husband is gone. I don't wait for that day because it's not going to happen. I realized many years ago it wasn't going to be solved. You just have to at some point move past that, because if you dwell on it, you'll take that anger to your grave."

When Sarah Salter arrived for work at A&B Sound on a cold winter morning in December 1995, all was normal until someone said her uncle had come by looking for her. Thinking that was odd, Sarah called her mother, Sheila, a half hour into her shift. The woman who answered the phone informed Sarah that her mother hadn't come in to work. She was missing, and the police had been to her mother's office, along with Sarah's dad.

"I crouched down on the floor behind the counter with the phone. I didn't know what to do," said Sarah. The phone conversation had made her feel sick to her stomach.

That morning, moments after forty-two-year-old Sheila arrived at the city parking garage near the west Edmonton business where she worked as a life coach, a man attacked and abducted her in her Chevy Blazer. The first blow, dealt by the attacker who tried to kill her by hurling himself from a dark corner, splattered blood on the Blazer's driver-side door. The assailant chased Sheila around the vehicle to the rear passenger door, then forced her inside.

Sheila was stabbed in the neck, causing a major wound to an artery. Her throat was also slashed. When she was nearly dead, her attacker pulled Sheila into the back of the vehicle and raped her. At around 5 p.m. that same day, the blood-soaked Blazer was found parked behind an apartment building downtown.

The following days were horrible for twenty-year-old Sarah, as she and her family waited anxiously for news about Sheila's whereabouts. They gathered at Sarah's aunt's house, waiting for something hopeful. That hope was shattered ten days later when homicide detectives delivered the news that Sheila's body had been found in an abandoned farmhouse near Chipman, seventy-five kilometres east of Edmonton. The knot that had been tightening in Sarah's stomach finally gave way. She walked into the bathroom and threw up repeatedly. The terrifying attack on an innocent woman left many Edmontonians shaken, including those investigating the crime.

"This case really took its toll on me," said Edmonton Police Constable Joe Slemko, one of the city's top bloodstain experts. "I had to walk in her last steps. I had to visualize what she saw, by looking at the blood stains."

The day after her mother's body was discovered, Sarah woke to see the sun shining. It was a beautiful day. Then she remembered what happened to her mother. Walks in the ravine or river valley no longer felt safe. The life Sarah had known now seemed gone forever.

"It was absolutely devastating," she said. "You are in survival mode. You get through each day not even knowing how."

It didn't take long before a man by the name of Peter Brighteyes was charged with Sheila's death and eventually convicted of first-degree murder. After the vicious assault, Brighteyes had taken a ring Sheila was wearing and sold it to buy alcohol and drugs. The ring was key in leading detectives to the identity of Sheila's killer and issuing warrants for his arrest.

Brighteyes had been released from jail only four days prior to the deadly attack. By this point in his life, correctional facilities were a place the violent offender had come to know well. In 1984 Brighteyes had been sentenced to eight years in prison for the horrific seven-hour torture and mutilation of a guard at the Peace River Correctional Centre. Nine years later he was handed a two-year sentence for the unconscionable knife attack, beating, and robbery of a man he befriended at an Edmonton hotel. The victim was stabbed in the stomach and suffered injuries to his eyes and liver.

In April 1997, Brighteyes was handed a life sentence for Sheila's murder, but he only served one day of that sentence. The convicted killer hanged himself from a collapsible coat hook, jury-rigged to hold his 141 pounds. The thirty-five-year-old had committed more than thirty crimes since the age of sixteen.

Sarah waded numbly through the first year of living without her mother. She couldn't talk to her friends about the murder, but she refused to be a victim. Eventually Sarah found her own ways to deal with her grief and gradually came to a place of reconciliation.

"I wasn't sitting there holding onto it. If I got upset or angry, I would go and scream. If I felt sad, I would go for a walk in the ravine and cry and sing. I would always be doing something to get that energy out," said Sarah, who felt more comfortable talking about her mother's death five years later.

It took another five years before she was able to openly discuss with strangers how her mother died. Now, as a ceremonialist, teacher, and spiritual healer, she helps others who are dealing with trauma to cope with their pain. Talking about murder is something she no longer hides.

When Sarah thinks about her mother, she remembers a woman who had an amazing capacity to elicit a sense of wonderment and playfulness through her approach to life. One summer morning when Sarah was fifteen years old, her mother left her a note with some chores. In that note was a long description of how to properly wash and wax the linoleum floors. Feeling confused and somewhat ticked off, Sarah phoned her mother at work, looking for an explanation.

"She was saying, 'Isn't this so exciting? You've never learned how to do that before.' Even if it was a task like washing floors you could have fun and like it if you wanted to, and I applied that philosophy to a lot of things," said Sarah, adding that becoming a mother herself helped with her healing.

"I'm never going to be happy that my mom's dead. She was one of the most amazing teachers and beings in my life, but I can't change [the fact that she died]. I can be stuck and not talk about it—and then you have continuously a yuck feeling in the pit of your stomach or throat—or we can talk about these things, so that's what I do."

There is nothing more terrifying than when a stranger attacks an innocent person going about their daily routine. Sheila Salter fell victim to this horrific experience. So did Cathy Greeve.

On the afternoon of August 3, 1988, Cathy met her husband, Tony, for lunch at Earl's in downtown Edmonton. When the couple finished dining, they walked back to Tony's van, parked outside city hall, where Cathy gave him an affectionate kiss before heading to the Churchill LRT station. It was the last time Tony would ever see his wife alive.

Shortly after the lunch date, the twenty-nine-year-old was found, semi-clad, with no pulse, slumped over a toilet in the women's washroom at the LRT station. A pair of pantyhose was wrapped twice loosely around her throat and attached to the handicap rail in the bathroom stall. Blood was on the wall, floor, and countertop by one of the sinks.

Cathy's blouse was open, her bra pulled up to expose one breast. Her skirt was also missing, along with a few of her personal belongings. An autopsy later revealed that Cathy had suffered two blunt-force blows to the back of her head, but her death was ultimately caused by ligature strangulation with the pantyhose.

The horrific crime left Cathy's family bearing the wounds of grief, anguish, and oppressive sadness. Cathy's father, Martin Hattersley, was a part-time Anglican priest and a successful lawyer with three daughters. He was having lunch with a client when he heard the news that a young woman had been murdered in the bathroom of an Edmonton transit station. Hours later, he found out the young woman was his daughter.

"A loss like this comes as a stunning blow to anyone who suffers it, and our first reaction was of disbelief—such things are not supposed to happen to an office worker downtown in the middle of Edmonton in the middle of the working day," said Martin, who began questioning his faith in God.

Tony and the couple's two children, aged eight and six, moved out of their rented Edmonton home. The grieving husband couldn't bear living in the same house where he and Cathy had been dreaming and planning their future. The children then went to live with Tony's parents in Lamont, Alberta, going to school in the neighbouring community of Fort Saskatchewan, while their father waded through a fog of grief.

With a killer now on the loose, police began looking at Tony as a suspect, which is a common practice when a spouse is murdered. Homicide detectives interrogated Tony for weeks, even taking him into the washroom where Cathy died to see how he'd react. Eventually, it got to the point where people would leave restaurants when they recognized him, thinking he was the killer.

"They were as cruel, cold, and calculating as the criminals they catch," said Tony about the detectives.

A little more than two months after Cathy was killed, Ronald Nienhuis was arrested after a botched bank robbery, in which he dropped most of the money and ran past the getaway vehicle without seeing it. The young man was fingerprinted at Edmonton Police headquarters. The right thumbprint matched that taken from the toilet where Cathy's body was found, leaving Nienhuis with an additional charge of first-degree murder.

News of an arrest came as a shock for Tony. He wasn't aware police even had a suspect. "I was more prepared for police to bring all the inconsistencies together and grill me," he said. "I was relieved."

Following the arrest, more details about Nienhuis's activities in the days leading up to Cathy's untimely death began to unfold. Two weeks before the slaying, the National Parole Board of Canada had granted Nienhuis day parole to assist with his integration back into the community after he had served half of a six-year sentence for four bank robberies. He was allowed to leave the Belmont Correctional Centre during the day and return at night, where he was confined in a dormitory. Despite a troubling track record, the board did not perceive Nienhuis as an undue risk or a violent person. Nienhuis, however, had been drinking heavily every day since entering the correctional centre, including the day he met Cathy at the LRT station.

During a fourteen-hour interview with police, Nienhuis initially denied killing Cathy, arguing he was a bank robber, not a murderer. But after twelve hours—although he had difficulty remembering what he did the day Cathy was killed—he finally admitted to the crime, claiming it was an "accident."

Nienhuis told the detective he saw and spoke to Cathy near the woman's washroom in the LRT station. He found her attractive and thought she was trying to hide her wedding ring during the brief conversation. Thinking maybe she liked him, Nienhuis asked Cathy if she wanted to go for a drink or something. Then he made a bold move.

"I reached over and I gave her ass a feel. She screamed. So I put up my hand around her mouth. She kicked and started screaming louder," he told detectives, adding he was "stone-drunk" at the time.

Nienhuis grabbed Cathy by the throat and pushed her inside the women's washroom. "We were fighting all the way in there but I had a hold of her throat," he said. "I wanted to let go of her, but she wouldn't stop screaming. Man, I just grabbed her and pushed her against the wall. And she went down, and she didn't get back up."

In an act of desperation, Nienhuis said he took off his glasses and placed them in front of Cathy's mouth to see if she was breathing. But the lenses didn't fog up, leading Nienhuis to assume the young woman he was just chatting with was suddenly dead.

Fearing police would see the crime the wrong way, Nienhuis said he propped Cathy's body up on the toilet seat, but she kept falling off so he tied pantyhose around her neck to keep her upright. He took a few of Cathy's belongings to make it look like a robbery. Her skirt and panties were also taken, and her bra was left askew to fool police.

"I took all that with me 'cause I figured that, you know, maybe they'll blame it on a sex crime or somethin' like that," said Nienhuis, adding that he raced out of the washroom and dumped the items he'd taken under a bush down the hill from the Chateau Lacombe Hotel downtown.

This was hardly the first time Nienhuis had found himself in trouble with the law. The career criminal had twenty-four previous convictions, a long record of internal prison offences, and had yet to complete half of his sentence for multiple bank robberies when Cathy was killed. Repeating his past, Nienhuis quickly became a problematic prisoner at the Edmonton Institution, facing internal charges for fighting with another inmate, possession of drugs, and being drunk or under the influence of drugs.

Ten years earlier, Nienhuis had been diagnosed as a budding anti-social personality type (psychopath) who was manipulative and showed a lack of remorse and concern for his victims. Even the foster mother who once adopted Nienhuis told a probation officer he should not be out in society unless he'd received a tremendous amount of treatment. He was removed from the home at age twelve after the family physician suggested he might kill someone.

"Whenever he did something wrong, he never showed any remorse," said the adoptive mother in a pre-sentence report. "He just didn't seem to care about the feelings of anyone when he did something bad."

Psychiatrists further deemed Nienhuis an extremely angry and hostile individual. His behaviour had escalated from that which he displayed during early childhood, and it was unlikely to ever change.

During the trial, Nienhuis demonstrated a variety of behaviours. The accused killer hung his head and twice wiped tears from his eyes when his videotaped confession to police was played before the packed courtroom. On one day, Nienhuis repeatedly nodded off, occasionally talking in his sleep before tumbling out of the prisoner's box onto his face and passing out. On another day, Nienhuis exploded with rage at Crown prosecutor Gary McCuaig, cursing, shouting, and hurling a pen at his head. The emotional outburst came during final arguments, as Gary tore into Nienhuis's version of how he killed Cathy. The prosecutor rejected Nienhuis's claim that the killing was an accident, stating the twenty-five-year-old's story was self-serving and that parts of it were totally unbelievable.

Court of Queen's Bench Justice Joanne Veit found Nienhuis guilty of manslaughter instead of first-degree murder, because she had a reasonable doubt he intended to kill the young woman. Justice Veit said placing the nylon around an unconscious woman's neck was clearly an act of criminal negligence, but she doubted it was purposely done to kill Cathy, as the Crown alleged.

"If the accused wanted to kill Ms. Greeve, why would he place a loose ligature around her neck? Why would he not use a slip knot to achieve his objective?" she asked.

Tony buried his face in his hands for much of the judge's remarks. Outside the courtroom, he described his reaction as absolute shock.

"I thought there was enough evidence for first-degree murder," Tony said. The decision also came as a surprise to Cathy's father.

"I think he has been given the benefit of every possible doubt in this case," Martin said. The Crown later appealed the case, calling for a verdict of murder instead of manslaughter.

In the months leading up to the sentencing hearing, a handful of things happened around the city in light of Cathy's death. New security systems were installed in the LRT stations to increase passenger safety. The changes included lock controls in all washrooms so anyone wanting to use the facilities would have to use an intercom to ask security staff to open doors.

More than 250 people also took part in a block-long procession for International Women's Day. It was the biggest turnout yet. The group chose to mark Cathy's death because the killer was convicted of manslaughter instead of murder. They stood quietly as a white rose was placed near the scene of the murder. The rose was a symbol of the hurt, anger, and fear women were feeling.

As for Tony, he was not only living a nightmare, he was experiencing them as well. He would dream that nothing bad had happened, then wake up to the devastating realization that Cathy was gone forever.

"The life I was living came to a very abrupt end, and I had to start a new life again," he said. "It's been like living in a nightmare. You have to find ways of coping with it."

Nienhuis showed no emotion as he was sentenced to twenty-three-and-a-half-years behind bars for Cathy's senseless death. Another eight-year sentence was added for the bank robbery, giving him a total of thirty-one-and-a-half-years behind bars. It was one of the stiffest sentences ever

Martin Hattersley, with a portrait of his daughter, is overcome with emotion as he speaks to a reporter in his west-end Edmonton home in September 2010. Cathy Greeve was murdered in 1988. (Photo by David Bloom / Courtesy of Sun Media)

given for manslaughter in Alberta. Nienhuis later appealed his sentence, but the Alberta Court of Appeal raised his penalty to life in prison.

More than twenty years later, Martin Hattersley bears Nienhuis no ill will, nor does he take any comfort or satisfaction in knowing the killer is behind bars. The family has had to find their own way through their grief, and it hasn't been easy. Cathy's mother, Florence, has battled depression ever since her daughter was killed. Sometimes the sadness has been so overwhelming she's been hospitalized. Martin's own road to recovery began when he learned to release his grief physically through shadow boxing in the basement.

Although he will never see his smart and talented daughter again, Martin has put his terrible experience to good use by helping found the Victims of Homicide Support Society. He continues to sit on the board, teaching other homicide victims how to forgive.

"I was very angry with God," he said. "If you believe that everything that happens is God's unfolding of the universe, when something like this happens, you start to wonder, what the hell is God doing?"

Martin finds it interesting that Nienhuis has been eligible for parole but declines to apply. "He's been a product of the system since he was twelve years old," he said. "It's what he knows."

Mir Hussain's family often urged him to quit his job. Working at an Impark parking lot, he received on-the-job threats and was sometimes chased down by drivers angry about parking tickets. But his family never dreamed that Mir's job could cost him his life.

It was just after 8 p.m. on January 2, 2004, when the forty-four-year-old was stopped for a traffic light in his 1997 Toyota Corolla at the intersection of 121st Street and 104th Avenue. A witness saw him arguing outside the car with another person, who may have come from an older model hatchback parked behind Mir's car. Sometime during the argument, Mir was stabbed in the torso. He managed to stop another car for help and was taken to a nearby pizza business to wait for an ambulance. His last words were prayers he said in the ambulance before losing consciousness and passing away twenty-four hours later.

It didn't take long before police were standing on Mir's doorstep, telling his wife, Bushra, that she needed to come to the hospital because her husband had been stabbed. But it was too late; he was already slipping away.

"I wanted to speak to him, but he wasn't there, he was unconscious. All we [saw was] him lying there with all the machines around him," remembered Bushra, following the ten-year anniversary of her husband's death. "That day he left for work, that's the last time he said good-bye. I never thought in my wildest nightmare that he would never come back."

Following the death of Mir (known by friends and family as Fareed), Impark offered a $5,000 reward for information leading to an arrest, and a trust fund was also set up for his family. Police have a description of the suspect—a Caucasian or Native male, five-foot-ten to six-feet tall, with a medium build. He was wearing dark sweat-style pants, a black toque, and a black and white parka at the time of the attack, but no suspect has yet been arrested and charged.

Abdulaziz Quraishi often asked his cousin—who was a pathologist before moving to Canada from India—to change careers. Abdulaziz heard Mir recount several incidents about being chased by angry drivers after he had given them parking tickets. He once had his nose broken by someone he ticketed in a parking lot near Whyte Avenue. But despite the risks, Mir saw the advantages of the job.

"It freed up his time during the day to devote to his kids and his wife," said Abdulaziz. "He was in a Catch-22 situation. He was making a living writing tickets. At the same time, it was something that was not positive for [him]."

Mir's death left Bushra in the clutches of uncontrollable grief. She was in the midst of recovering from cancer treatments, so things had been looking up for the family, which had also been recovering from a terrible tragedy five years earlier. In 1999 one of the couple's daughters was the sole survivor of a car crash near Drumheller that claimed the lives of four other family members. The accident left the girl permanently disabled. Their two other children, a girl and boy, were aged ten and three at the time of their father's death. Bushra was left to raise them on her own.

It took about a month before the Hussain family grew frustrated by the investigation, claiming that police hadn't caught the killer because the case didn't involve a high-profile individual. Police insisted, however, that they were anxious to solve the homicide but the investigation was complicated: it involved an attack by a stranger, the vehicle description wasn't complete, and there weren't many witnesses who could give detectives concrete information.

"The saddest part is there were witnesses there, the description of the vehicle and the licence plate and what have you. So that kind of makes the family feel empty inside as to how people get away with doing these things," said Mir's cousin, Syed Rahman, in February 2004. "The family just feels the matter has been shoved in the back. Law enforcement is not doing as much as they should."

Mir came to Canada in 1990 from India, where he and Bushra had met and fallen in love. Bushra describes her husband of fifteen years as a real gentleman. When asked to provide anecdotes to help describe Mir, she said she had too many good memories of her time with him to choose from.

"He used to give me door-to-door service if I went out with him. He treated me like a queen all the time," she said, her voice shaky. "He was a very caring husband, a very caring father, and a dear friend that I could always count on."

Bushra couldn't believe when ten years had passed and the killer had not yet been found. She worried the case had been forgotten, which left her feeling angry and sad. Her youngest son has lived his life without a father, and graduations have come and gone. Mir's death is in her thoughts every day, and she continues to wait for closure.

"The things I've been through, nobody can experience that," she said. "It's very sad for us still. Nobody can fulfill the loss that I have and my children are feeling today. I want justice. I want to know why he did that. Why did he choose my husband out of the blue—one innocent person. They took his life and affected four other lives so badly. We wrack our brains and sit here and speculate. There are so many questions that need to be answered."

I t was a day that started off just like any other. Bundled up with her nine-month-old baby boy, Vera Stortz was dropped off at around 7:30 a.m. at the west Edmonton home of Jack and Vivian Murrell to babysit her young niece, Tania, and nephew, John. It was something she had been doing for the last three years.

Tania was having a lively conversation with her mother about the outfit she had selected to wear to school that day in January 1983. The six-year-old settled on her black Harley-Davidson T-shirt and green corduroy pants to wear to her Grade 1 class.

Jack headed off for his job with a homebuilder, while Vivian left shortly after for her manager job at a nearby bakery. Vera asked Tania and John what they wanted for lunch that day. The pair both replied—macaroni and cheese.

"I love you," said Vera as she gave the pair a hug before they walked out the front door for the nearby Grovenor School, two-and-a-half blocks from their home.

Just before 11 a.m., Vera began to prepare lunch. The front door opened twenty minutes later. Vera called out, but only John replied.

"It's just me. Tania's not with me," he said.

Instead of waiting the ten minutes for John's dismissal from kindergarten so the pair could walk home together for lunch, Tania had waved goodbye to two classmates at school and marched off alone toward 144th Street.

"Tania said she had some money and she was going to the 7-Eleven for lunch," said her friend Brandy-Jo Ewashko, who turned down Tania's offer to join her because her mother had scolded her the previous day for not waiting for her brother.

"I never did see any money and did not know if Tania was going to meet someone or not," Brandy-Jo said. "I do know she wasn't going home for lunch."

Given that Tania was reliable about being on time, Vera began to feel uneasy as more time passed by. She called Vivian to let her know that Tania hadn't come home for lunch. Other students had told John his sister went to a friend's home, so Vera bundled up her baby and hurried to the friend's house, which was just at the end of the street. But Tania wasn't there. Vera was filled with worry.

Tania wasn't in class either when school resumed after lunch. Aside from a Safeway bag she left at school, there was no sign of the bubbly, blonde-haired, brown-eyed girl anywhere on the property. The family called police and dug up pictures of the missing girl, showing them to neighbours as they went door to door.

The mysterious disappearance of a beautiful young child sparked the largest search ever mounted in the city at that time. Hundreds of volunteers came forward, covering more than 1,900 square blocks in the following days, including alleys and ravines. Two anonymous city businessmen offered $30,000 to anyone who found Tania alive.

A witness later reported seeing a little girl matching Tania's description being dragged across 144th Street near 104th Avenue around 11:15 a.m. by a woman between the ages of forty and sixty. It was the second report police received about the incident and the strongest lead they had to go on, despite more than a thousand calls to their special information line.

"We are anxious to trace this woman," said a city police spokesperson. "It is possible she could have been collecting a child from school and is not involved in Tania's disappearance. Even so we would like to talk to her so we could rule her out of our investigation."

Citizens at search headquarters also received a mystery telephone call from a young girl who asked for her mommy and identified herself as Tania. The phone line went dead seconds into the call, leaving detectives unable to confirm if the girl was indeed the young child.

The strain of missing their beloved little girl clamped down on Tania's worried parents. Jack tried going back to his job twenty-four days after Tania disappeared, but he found it emotionally trying. Vivian had yet to even try going back to work. Their young son John refused to sleep in the bunk bed he used to share with his sister.

"I've taken him in there when he's been asleep but as soon as he wakes up, he gets out. He's scared," said Jack. "It's getting worse for us, the longer it gets. It's almost like some terrible movie on TV. It's hard to believe it's real."

A few days after Jack's attempt to go back to work, a man called civilian search headquarters and told a volunteer the search for Tania was over. The mystery caller said, "I've got her and I want to talk to Jack." He was given the Murrells' number and called Jack minutes later, asking for the now $40,000 reward.

"He sounded sincere. This guy had the perfect story," said Jack. "I believed him."

The Murrells spent a sleepless night anguishing over the latest development in the case, but at noon the next day the man was arrested downtown and charged with extortion.

"That's a terrible thing to do. I hope that guy never sees the light of day again," said Jack. "This one really hurt. We had everything riding on it. We honestly thought we were going to have our little girl home again."

As the days turned into weeks, police were almost certain someone had abducted the young child. Superintendent Leroy Chahley publically appealed to the abductor to leave Tania somewhere warm, such as a shopping mall, then phone police anonymously to say where she was. He also appealed to the abductor's family (in case they knew anything or had any suspicions) to phone and help police with the investigation. In the absence of any solid leads, police studied the files of possible suspects and made background checks on family and friends.

"We're not ruling out any possibility," Leroy said.

Two days into March, an emotional Vivian pleaded with the Edmonton Police Commission to step up search tactics and consider calling the armed forces. She believed psychic reports that Tania was still alive and being held in a house in or near the city.

"Why can't the army be brought in?" she asked. "Why can't every abandoned building and home in Edmonton be checked? What does it take to have something done? If I have to, I'll go through every house in the city and look for her myself. I'm not going to wait. You can't possibly tell me she's not out there somewhere. Do you expect me to wait a year?"

Vivian's pleas, however, were unsuccessful.

Five days later, police broke with tradition and called famous Illinois seer Greta Alexander, who was known for her success in solving mysteries. But this proved fruitless.

Police also gave polygraph tests to Tania's parents, and Vera and her common-law husband, even though they were never considered suspects.

On Tania's seventh birthday, her family left town for a few days and went to a lakeside resort to mark the occasion with a simple ceremony. Nobody sang, gave Tania presents, or wished her well. The only wishes were that the birthday girl would some day come home to her heartbroken family, safe and sound.

"My mind tells me Tania is dead, but my heart says she's alive," said Vivian. "And until we find out otherwise I have to go with what my heart feels. It's only right." Not a day goes by when Vivian doesn't plunge into a deep depression for at least a few hours.

"The only thing I can do is keep busy," she said. "But there are times—especially at night—when I can't help but think of Tania. When I'm cleaning the house I have to be careful I don't go into the closet where I keep all of Tania's clothes. Otherwise I'll just drop to the ground and cry for hours."

Tania's disappearance sparked the formation of the Missing Children Society of Canada—a non-profit group linked to dozens of similar agencies in the U.S., all looking for missing children. It was the only Canadian-based support group for missing kids and their families at the time. If a child went missing, the society could have information and pictures sent out to the various agencies within hours. Getting involved with the foundation kept Vivian from going crazy.

As the investigation continued, city detectives continued to be just as baffled as anyone else about the case. There were no traces of her clothing or schoolbooks. Tania seemed to have vanished off the face of the Earth.

"We don't know anything more today than we did the day Tania went missing. She has vanished without a trace," said Homicide Detective John McLeod, who had many sleepless nights, sometimes getting up at 4 a.m. to work on the case in his head.

By the time the one-year anniversary of Tania's disappearance rolled around, police had more than two thousand tips from Alaska to Zimbabwe and had interviewed nearly four thousand people from across North America, but nothing advanced the case. Tips from 379 psychics also failed to yield any substantial leads.

Detectives occasionally received reports of possible Tania sightings. An Ontario woman on vacation in the Queen Charlotte Islands thought she'd seen a girl who matched Tania's description, but with hair dyed red. Due to the sparsely populated area, police were able to determine that Tania was not there.

One time, the Murrells had high hopes of being reunited with their daughter when they received a phone call from the Society for Young Victims in Newport, Rhode Island, with information about a possible sighting. Vivian was told that a woman in Arizona thought she recognized Tania from a photo on a television broadcast. The girl had many of Tania's physical characteristics, but the one thing that stood out was that one of the names of the girl's dogs was Harley—the same name as Tania's old dog. The girl was also ambidextrous, increasing the Murrells' optimism.

American officials had all the documentation and photographs of the girl thought to be Tania waiting for Vivian when she arrived, but she immediately knew the girl wasn't her missing daughter.

Tania's picture also appeared on NBC's *Today Show* and on *Adam*—a made-for-television movie about a Florida boy found murdered. She was the only Canadian young-ster featured among forty-three missing children on the post-show list that was seen in millions of homes across Canada and the United States. The telecast resulted in thirteen of the featured children being returned to their homes, but Tania wasn't one of them.

Nearly two years after Tania disappeared, the Murrells welcomed a baby girl into their family. They eventually moved to B.C.'s Okanagan, but they couldn't erase the stress of their missing child, and they turned to booze and drugs to escape the thoughts whirling through their heads. The couple wound up contracting hepatitis C, leading to long-term health problems for both of them, and they divorced in the 1990s.

Despite their differences, Vivian and Jack worked for decades to keep Tania's disappearance in the spotlight. Fighting back from the crippling effects of a massive brain aneurysm, Vivian vowed to never give up until Tania was found.

"Somebody knows something. We don't just get picked up and thrown in the garbage," she said. "Are we sup-posed to just sweep Tania under the rug? Even though it's been years, they should be able to solve this case. As far as I'm concerned, this [case] is overly cold."

Vivian is critical of a lot of things police did during the course of their investigation. At one point, detectives identified an old family acquaintance as a suspect in the young girl's disappearance, but no arrest was ever made. Vivian also questioned why police never searched the area of Cooking Lake east of Edmonton, where she had come to believe Tania could likely be found.

With nothing to go on for so many years, Vivian turned to psychics for information, one of whom said Tania was hit over the head with a rock and died. Imagining such a violent death is painful. Instead, Vivian likes to think Tania could still be happy and alive somewhere.

"I still look for her. I don't care if it sounds crazy, but a mother knows her child so I have to at least look for her," said Vivian. "I often think of my little Tania when she was six years old, and she's wearing her beautiful little red dress and she's over my shoulder and we're laughing. I smile at her every day, but it's still very painful and it's still very difficult. The tears are still there."

For ten days in the summer of 2008, it looked like Edmonton Police had finally caught the break they had been waiting for. Detectives took the unusual step of digging up part of a basement in a home twenty blocks from where the Murrells used to live. The search was sparked following a tip in 2007 from a woman who had been a casual playmate of Tania. The woman made allegations of sexual abuse against her father, whom she believed could have been responsible for the young girl's death. Always suspicious of her estranged father, the woman decided it was finally time to come forward.

"She called us to say at the time Tania disappeared there was a hole in the basement room at their house," said Detective Howie Antoniuk of the historical homicide unit. "She understood [the hole] had been left for some plumbing work."

The family living upstairs in the home and the tenants living in the basement were put up in a hotel as detectives moved in to investigate. A police-hired contractor broke through the floor. The concrete underneath appeared to be disturbed, piquing Howie's interest.

Police dug half a metre down and examined the area for any trace of human remains, but everything came back negative. There had never been a body in or under the basement's concrete floor. Nonetheless, police still approached the woman's estranged father, who took a polygraph test and passed.

Thirty years after Tania disappeared, tips in the case had become extremely rare. In 2012, Howie received just one tip, allowing him time to finish transferring thousands of files and documents from the case onto a disc—a process that took two years.

One man remaining on police radar who has yet to be eliminated as a suspect is a friend of the family who helped in the search for the young girl. The man was working outdoors on the morning of January 20, 1983, and can't independently prove where he was. He took a polygraph test, but the results were inconclusive. A few months after Tania vanished, the man and his wife moved to Ontario. A cloud of suspicion still hangs over him due to some

Edmonton Police Detective Howie Antoniuk holds a poster with information about Tania Murrell, who went missing on January 20, 1983. (Tania's last name was misspelled on this handout.) (Photo by David Bloom / Courtesy of Sun Media)

strange things he said and wrote. Investigators, however, could neither confirm nor deny that he was involved.

"I would love nothing better than to solve this case before I retire. It has been so long," said Howie, who believes Tania is dead. "My gut feeling is she is not alive. I believe she was murdered and her body disposed of shortly after she disappeared, probably in a dumpster."

Vivian wished to get some answers about her missing daughter before she died, but she passed away on New Year's Day in January 2011 at the age of fifty-five from ongoing health problems. Jack had passed away six years earlier from kidney failure.

Tania's disappearance was especially tough on her brother, John, who was very close to his big sister. Once she was gone, the focus was always on finding Tania, leaving John feeling neglected. By the age of thirty-five, John had been in and out of B.C. jails most of his adult life due to a bad drug habit. He was incarcerated again in 2012 after a high-speed chase that injured an RCMP officer near Revelstoke. In 2015, John was found dead in an Edmonton halfway house. An autopsy failed to determine the cause of death.

This leaves Tania's younger sister, Elysia, not even alive when Tania disappeared, to continue the search for the family's missing loved one.

Elysia became a nurse as a tribute to the sister she never met and who she believes is still alive. Each year on the anniversary of Tania's disappearance, Elysia walks to nearby Niagara Falls with her children and throws in a red rose.

"Before my dad passed away, he told me he was going to see my sister," she said. "I told him, you won't find her because she's not there."

Tania's disappearance has also had a deep impact on her aunt and one-time babysitter, Vera Stortz, who raised three sons with her common-law husband. The couple was ultra-paranoid with their children, having them report their whereabouts at all times. More than thirty years later, the mystery of what happened to her niece still haunts her. "I think about Tania every day," she said. "I am still hoping she comes home."

Tania's case is now one of the coldest missing child cases in Canadian history, occupying more than 20,000 pages of police files. Her disappearance also sparked the creation of the first Alberta chapter of Child Find, and it continues to serve as a reminder to parents to empower their children with knowledge of what to do in the face of danger and how to avoid it.

PROJECT KARE

The Christmas of 1996 is a holiday season Mary Willier would like to forget, but she can't, no matter how hard she tries. The sixty-four-year-old knew something was wrong when her daughter, Joanne Ghostkeeper, failed to show up for Christmas dinner with her children that year. During Mary's last conversation with her daughter, twenty-four-year-old Joanne talked about how excited she was to be spending Christmas with her family and how she hoped her children would enjoy their gifts, but those gifts were never delivered.

When there was no word from her daughter, Mary phoned her ex-husband, asking him to go to Joanne's east-side apartment and see if she was there. There was no response, so he phoned the police, who found the vibrant mother of two strangled with an electrical cord in her fourth-floor suite at 11925 34th Street.

Joanne was last seen drinking at the Beverly Crest Motel two days before with another woman and a few men. The group was cut off by the bartender and they moved on. What happened to Joanne after that remains a mystery.

When Mary thinks about her daughter, her voice starts to quiver, and her eyes fill with tears. "It just lingers every minute of the day. I remember how she used to laugh and have fun," said Mary. "We haven't had a good Christmas since then."

Police maintain that the case is still active and they continue to investigate any leads regarding Joanne's untimely death. She was known to live a high-risk lifestyle, and she is one of more than a dozen sex-trade workers found slain in and around Edmonton within two decades. Since 1975, the bodies of at least thirty women, many of them prostitutes, have been found in the Edmonton region. Dozens more are still listed as missing. Many of the cases remain unsolved.

Staff Sergeant Gerard MacNeil is among a handful of Mounties dedicated to finding the person or persons responsible for cutting short the lives of these women. He's convinced a serial killer was, and still may be, on the loose.

"Certainly from the patterns that we've investigated on many of these offences, we know that there was a serial offender at work, and we haven't caught him," said Gerard. "I can't say whether that person is alive, whether they are in custody for other offences, or whether they have left the province. For whatever reason, they have simply gone dormant."

Gerard works with Project KARE, an RCMP subunit of "K" Division's Serious Crime Branch, which was formed in June 2003 to investigate the deaths of women living high-risk lifestyles. The term "high risk" doesn't necessarily relate only to sex-trade workers, but also to women who associate with certain circles and participate in certain activities that put them at a higher risk of being victims of crime. At the time of KARE's formation, there were eighty-three cases of women who had gone missing under suspicious circumstances, six of which had met with foul play. Evidence found in those six cases suggested the killings were committed by the same person or people.

Despite KARE's formation, the slayings continued. In 2003 four sex-trade workers were slain within a seven-month period. During the next two years, more women went missing, and four more mutilated and decomposing bodies surfaced in fields on the eastern edge of the city. The slayings eventually tapered off in 2006; ten lives were taken by 2007.

Kate Quinn, with the Centre to End All Sexual Exploitation (CEASE), felt angry and overwhelmed when two women were murdered within a few weeks of each other in January 2003, prior to KARE's formation. As the killings intensified, so did the fear among the women trolling the tracks between 166th and 133rd Street looking for a date—many to feed their addictions or to support drug-addicted boyfriends, others to buy food or diapers for their children.

"We call these the really terrible years," said Kate. "There were so many murders, one after another. It's significant that we have not had the high number of murders that we had between 2003 and 2006."

When KARE detectives aren't investigating cold-case murders, they hit the streets two to four times a week to connect with sex-trade workers. The proactive unit has registered more than 1,200 Alberta women living high-risk lifestyles. Registration includes name, address, a DNA sample, and a photo. Public health personnel are also on hand with officers to provide current information on the supports available to women who want to escape life on the street. Such measures have made it easier for officers to keep tabs on the women's whereabouts.

Gerard recalls how things were before KARE was formed: "Their support network [was] almost non-existent. Some of the girls were missing for weeks. [They'd] hang out with friends...do drugs with friends and [would be] very transient in or around the city. A lot of them [knew] each other only by street names." But with KARE, Gerard states, "If we get a report of a missing person we can fan the info out now to more than one hundred separate groups. It's a huge help."

Gerard couldn't say how many investigations KARE was involved in in 2012, but he noted it's fewer than fifty. Many files have already been picked apart by other police agencies, leaving KARE investigators the task of looking to see if things were missed or if something can be revisited using new technology. The bulk of the files are on women who have been found dead and who met with foul play, but there are still a large number of missing women that KARE is assisting to find.

Resources, however, aren't what they used to be. During the height of the slayings, more than fifty officers worked with KARE. By 2012 those numbers dwindled to about sixteen. Edmonton Police joined KARE in 2005 with four full-time investigators, but the police have since moved those positions back to their historical homicide unit.

The task force was originally given a three-year mandate, but investigators continue to follow up with dozens of persons of interest who Gerard suspects are capable of committing heinous crimes. So far, only two men—Joseph Laboucan and Thomas Svekla—have been brought to justice for two of the slayings.

Svekla, a forty-year-old Edmonton mechanic who once called himself the Robert Pickton of Alberta, was the first person charged as a result of Project KARE. In May 2006, Svekla brought a hockey bag from his High Level apartment to his sister's home in Fort Saskatchewan, just east of Edmonton. When questioned about the heavy bag, Svekla told his sister that it contained earth and compost worms, but she had a hard time believing him. His sister eventually opened the bag and discovered a body tightly wrapped in an air mattress, garbage bags, and a shower curtain held together by 58 small-gauge wires. The body was so badly decomposed that the medical examiner was unable to determine the cause of death but believed it had been frozen for some time.

The remains were identified as Theresa Innes, a crack addict and sex-trade worker in the northern Alberta town of High Level. Although she was never seen drinking anything stronger than coffee, thirty-six-year-old Theresa was a regular in the bars, appearing several times a week, but by March 2006 she hadn't been seen in months and was eventually reported missing.

Svekla was convicted of second-degree murder and handed a life sentence with no-chance of parole for seventeen years. He was also found guilty of offering an indignity to a body.

During the same trial, Svekla was acquitted on identical charges in the 2004 death of prostitute Rachel Quinney. Svekla claimed he found the nineteen-year-old's mutilated, naked body while smoking crack with another prostitute in a wooded farmer's field near Fort Saskatchewan in June 2004, and he waited two days before reporting the discovery to police.

Investigators suspected Svekla of killing as many as twelve prostitutes, but he was only ever charged with the two murders—Theresa's and Rachel's. Deemed by psychiatrists as a "highly psychopathic, violent individual," Svekla was designated a dangerous offender in May 2010. Joseph Laboucan wasn't much different.

In 2005, Laboucan and two other people lured thirty-three-year-old Ellie May Meyer to a farmer's field near Fort Saskatchewan for sex before she was beaten to death.

Addicted to crack cocaine, Ellie was working as a prostitute on Edmonton's 118th Avenue, turning tricks to support her habit. Her body was found a month later by a farmer tilling a field just east of Edmonton.

An autopsy showed Ellie suffered a fatal blow to her head, and the top of her left pinkie finger was missing. Laboucan later showed Ellie's finger, which he kept in a freezer between two pieces of bread, to a female accomplice, saying he wanted to kill again as it gave him an adrenalin rush.

Laboucan's DNA was found on Ellie's body, and in September 2011, he was convicted of first-degree murder and sentenced to life in prison without parole for twenty-five years. The twenty-six-year-old was already serving a life sentence for the rape and fatal beating of thirteen-year-old Nina Courtepatte, which occurred two days after Ellie was slain. Nina had been lured to the Edmonton Springs Golf Resort by a group of teens and young adults from nearby West Edmonton Mall on the promise they would take her to a rave. Instead, they drove her to the golf course, where she was raped twice, then beaten to death with a sledgehammer. Her body was found the next day on the fairway. In addition to Laboucan, four other people were put behind bars for the vicious crime.

Despite the low number of convictions related to the missing and murdered women, Gerard said that much of the success of Project KARE is that it has prevented more deaths from occurring.

"We are always making inroads, we are always learning new things," he said. "We would love to have brought resolution to more families, [but] these are very difficult, time-consuming, detailed investigations. They move very slowly, and quite often we will run up against a wall, and it's very frustrating to find a way over, around, or underneath the wall."

Kathy King is on the long list of people still waiting for a resolution. On September 1, 1997, the body of her only natural daughter, Cara, was found at the edge of a canola field near Sherwood Park and a bustling factory.

Cara was a free-spirited twenty-two-year-old who was very sociable and outgoing. She also loved to party, experimenting with drugs and hanging out with the wrong crowd, living a high-risk lifestyle.

Despite her mother's best efforts to help her, Cara became addicted to drugs and wound up working on the streets to pay for her habit. It was every parent's worst nightmare.

There's a lot about Cara's life on the streets that Kathy will never know, but her daughter always remained in touch. When Cara went missing in July 1997, Kathy began to fear the worst, and soon the nightmare intensified.

According to Kathy, the autopsy results were inconclusive, since only Cara's skeletal remains were found. After fifteen years, the person responsible for ending Cara's young life is still a mystery.

"She didn't take herself out to the middle of the field and beat herself up," Kathy said, adding, "It concerns me that the person responsible may still be out there. It concerns me that there are a number of people who are responsible for similar deaths that may still be out there." Speaking of Cara, Kathy said, "The grief is still there, the sadness is there, the regret is there. I think about her every day."

For the past nineteen years, Mary Willier has helped to raise Joanne's two children, who are now in their twenties. She suspects they are holding a lot of things in, and sometimes they question Mary about the mother they never had a chance to know. Mary tries her best to stay strong, but she admits that, at times, it's hard to control her emotions. One of the things that brings her comfort is a bag of her daughter's belongings she stores in her Edmonton home.

"I was thinking of going through them [the belongings] and maybe letting go, but I don't know if that would solve anything in my mind or in my heart," said Mary. "Sometimes I get so frustrated. I just start ripping things up. I don't know how much more I can plead to anyone."

In 2006, Mary found pictures of two men in her daughter's belongings. She handed the photos over to the investigators in the hope that these would help to solve the case. After releasing the photos to the public, police tracked down the two men and spoke with them, but they were ruled out as suspects.

Mary has suspicions about who killed her daughter and believes the case could easily be solved. But it's been years since she's heard anything from police, and her faith is dwindling every year her daughter's killer continues to walk free. She has even visited a psychic to try and get some answers to her many questions.

"I do remain hopeful, but I don't really have much faith with anything that they [the police] are doing," said Mary. "It's frustrating that they are not doing anything."

Every couple of months, Barb Kopf feels an urge to leave her Surrey, B.C., home for a few days and go to Edmonton. It's an urge she can't explain.

Ever since her seventeen-year-old daughter, Lisa, was found slain in a farmer's slough near Edmonton in August 1998, Barb hasn't been able to cut ties with Alberta's capital city, even though she wishes she could. The moment she's back in Edmonton, Barb is reminded of a pain so deep it instantly brings tears to her eyes. Yet she can't stay away.

"Every day, every moment, you wonder who's out there, and who did this to her, and how long they can live like this," said Barb, during a visit to Edmonton.

"I just don't think it's right to leave. I feel like I might be leaving her behind."

Barb and her two daughters, Lisa and Carla, moved from Victoria to Edmonton in 1997, with hopes of having a fresh start after her husband was killed by a drunk driver. Adjusting to life in a new city was difficult for the girls, but Barb said they were doing okay. That fresh start, however, was soon shattered to pieces.

On August 4, 1998, the two sisters left their Callingwood home in the city's west end for a house party near 102nd Street and 132nd Avenue in Lauderdale. They told their mom they'd take public transit to get back home. Shortly before midnight, Lisa called Barb to say they wouldn't make it to the LRT before it shut down for the night, so Barb told her to take a cab home with her sister. A couple of hours later, Carla arrived home alone. She couldn't find Lisa, and assumed she had already left the party.

"Right away I felt something was terribly wrong," said Barb, who got out the phone book and called every hospital and police station in the city, to no avail.

At 10 a.m. the next day, a farmer checking his cattle's watering hole on the outskirts of the city at 186th Street and 118th Avenue found Lisa's lifeless body, clad in track pants and a tank top. Police later confirmed that Lisa had left the house party around 4:30 a.m. and was believed to be walking home alone when she was killed. Toxicology tests showed no signs of alcohol or drugs in her system, confirming her death was not an accident. Someone had held her face in the mud until she suffocated.

Ernie Schreiber had just become a homicide detective with Edmonton Police when he was assigned to investigate Lisa's death. The day her body was discovered was the hottest day that summer, with temperatures skyrocketing to a scorching 34°C. The cows in the area had trampled the crime scene down significantly, creating a challenge for investigators. A footprint was found in the mud next to Lisa's body, but it wasn't defined enough to match to a shoe. Police did, however, manage to find a purse in the slough that contained Lisa's ID, and they notified her next of kin.

Ernie interviewed people who were at the house party on the night Lisa went missing. It was a rough crowd, he said, involving people who were drug dealers, some who've since passed away. Lisa didn't really know the people, but knew of them through her younger sister. At one point during the evening, Lisa decided that she had had enough and was going home.

"It could be something bothered her or upset her. We weren't able to determine that completely," said Ernie, adding a few people from the house later tried to find her, but had no success.

The morning Lisa was killed, police received a complaint about two suspicious vehicles—a white, two-door Toyota or Honda with blue blinking lights on its rear-view mirror, and a brand-new, teal-green, Japanese-made car—parked near an abandoned building in the same remote field where Lisa's body was found. Ernie believes the complaint might have been connected to Lisa's death or one of the people she was with at the party, but the connection is still unclear. One thing he is certain about is that more than one person was with Lisa at the time of her death.

"It would have been incredibly difficult for one individual just to be able to hold her down and to be able to make that happen without there being more signs of a struggle," said Ernie, adding Lisa was not a small girl. He also had some frustrations with her younger sister, Carla.

"She didn't cooperate at the very beginning, which for us was also a big red flag. You would think in a case where you discover your sister being murdered, you would do everything you can to cooperate and find out who did it. We had nothing but road blocks and were butting heads. I think there's a little bit of a story that she still knows, but won't talk about."

When police came to Barb's door the next day, she knew right away something terrible had happened to her daughter. The six months following Lisa's death are a blur. Shortly after Lisa's funeral, her favourite grandmother's heart gave out, adding one more burden to a family already wracked with grief.

Lisa had big dreams of becoming an actress some day. Her best friend described her as outgoing and intelligent, a perfect fit for achieving her dream, not a troubled teen as some might think. She also wanted to have a family of her own and had enrolled in high school to finish Grade 12 after taking a year off.

At this writing, over seventeen years have passed since the horrible crime, and the killer is still roaming free. With the right information, however, Ernie believes the case can still be solved.

"Homicide detectives work really hard to bring cases to a conclusion," he said, "but we also work with the understanding that, though we may have ideas and theories about how things will come about, sometimes that's out of our hands. You know the case will never ever die. [It] may sit on the shelf for a while until some new information comes in—you hope."

Barb Kopf holds a photo of her daughter, Lisa, who was murdered in 1998. (Photo by Jordan Verlage / Courtesy of Sun Media)

During the years, Barb has experienced a plethora of emotions. She spent the year after Lisa's death putting up posters in cities between Edmonton and Victoria, hoping someone would provide a break in the case. She still has hope that whoever killed her daughter will be brought to justice. That hope is what gets her through each day.

"I just want to find out who did this and why. I don't want people to forget this," said Barb, who still gets inquiries from strangers about Lisa's death. She can't help but think how things could have been different had she never moved to Edmonton.

"I just think, if I never brought my kids here, this would have never happened."

THE GRUESOME

On a crisp winter morning in December 2011, Luis Alvarado, the caretaker of a downtown apartment complex, received a phone call about a small leak coming from the roof of a first-floor storage unit below suite 205. The tenant in that suite, Joshua Houle, had previously experienced a problem with the dishwasher, but Luis had been told it was fixed.

Luis checked out the storage unit, which was packed with building supplies and furniture. He came across a puddle with a pinkish hue and heard the sound of running water coming from the suite above.

Luis contacted the suite manager to phone the tenant, but Houle couldn't be reached. With a fellow employee at his side, Luis went to Houle's suite, where he heard loud heavy-metal music muffling the sounds of splashing water. A low whir of a machine, like a blender or power tool, was also heard among the sounds of heavy guitar and thick bass. Although Houle didn't answer the door, Luis decided to go inside.

"When we cracked that door open, maybe seven inches wide, it felt like my heart stopped and just an adrenaline rush kicked in. We stepped back...in that instant, I see the walls are showered with blood," said Luis. "Same with the floors and the shoes that were scattered around. I immediately closed the door at that point and locked it."

Luis called police and soon found himself escorting two officers to the suite, where the water was still running and the heavy metal was playing at full blast. More knocks went unanswered, prompting Luis to open the door for the officers. This time he saw even more.

"I could see a leg. Not a full body, but a leg in the kitchen. It was in such an awkward spot that the fridge would have to be out of the way for the body to be there, and I didn't see the second leg," he said. "Not even the worst horror movie could depict or explain this...I was in complete shock and terrified."

It didn't take long for news to spread that the second-floor suite in the apartment complex along Jasper Avenue and 83rd Street was the scene of Edmonton's forty-seventh homicide that year, and it was a gruesome one. An autopsy confirmed that the victim was Misty Lynn Ward. The twenty-seven-year-old had died from a stab wound, and her remains were placed in Houle's bathtub filled with water, where the killer proceeded to cut and dismember her body.

A few days after the shocking crime, small white candles were placed beside a tree outside the apartment complex, along with pink and white flowers, cigarettes, and a few stuffed animals. It became a spot where family and friends gathered to remember a vibrant young woman who loved to laugh, play basketball, and watch the Edmonton Oilers.

"Didn't matter the mood. She'd walk in, and the room lit up," said one of Misty's cousins at her funeral. The ceremony attracted nearly two hundred mourners, who celebrated how Misty had lived rather than how she died.

"She liked to say, 'Live, laugh, love, and never give up.' She had a heart of gold," added the cousin.

Houle was charged with second-degree murder and with offering an indignity to human remains. The twenty-seven-year-old had just moved into the suite on December 23, and he was fired from his job at an autobody shop a week later. Since the shop rented the suite for employees, Houle had been asked to pack his bags.

Almost a year later, Houle admitted to fatally stabbing Misty in the neck. He pleaded guilty to a reduced charge of man-

Misty Lynn Ward. (Photo courtesy of Sun Media)

slaughter and offering an indignity to human remains. The court heard that Houle and Misty were friends who had known one another for years. There had never been a reason for Misty to fear for her safety.

On that fateful night in December, the pair met up and took a taxi to Houle's apartment. Surveillance cameras at the building showed they appeared to be in good spirits as they walked inside. The two drank and possibly used drugs before they had sex. Misty fell asleep on the bed, while Houle stayed up and drank beer. He later went out to purchase more booze.

Houle had previously warned Misty that he had a history of waking up violently if he was startled. He eventually fell asleep on the living room sofa. Some time later, Misty tried to wake him. Houle quickly jumped up and grabbed a serrated steak knife that was nearby, plunging it into the left side of Misty's neck. She moved around the suite with blood spurting out from her wound. It took Houle a few moments to realize what he had done.

A panicked Houle tried to help Misty by wrapping a towel around her neck and applying pressure, but the bleeding didn't stop. He put her in the bathtub, where she went into convulsions and eventually stopped moving.

When Houle couldn't find a pulse, he panicked, fearing that nobody would believe the killing of his friend was an accident. The only way out, he decided, was to get rid of her body.

Using the same steak knife, Houle cut off Misty's leg at the knee then placed it by the front door. He began cutting off her other leg but felt sick, so he went to lie down and fell asleep.

The tub began overflowing, the bloody water leaking through the floorboards into the storage room on the floor below. When police arrived and woke up Houle, he reacted violently then as well.

Houle was later handed an eight-year prison term—a sentence that didn't sit well with Misty's family.

"It's just a slap in the face—he is just laughing," said Misty's mother, Violet, outside of court. "It's just not right. Eight years for what he did to my baby. It's just not right. I am very upset."

The grisly crime shocked the city, but it wasn't the first time homicide detectives had come across a body that wasn't in one piece. A similarly chilling story unfolded just down the street four years prior to Misty's death. On February 21, 2007, the body of twenty-three-year-old David Wong was discovered slain and partially dismembered in a suite on the fourteenth floor of the Boardwalk Centre apartment building at 8820 Jasper Avenue.

David, who had ties to the drug trade, died as a result of multiple stab wounds—an estimated 158, mostly to his back. Police barged into the suite after a thirteenth-floor tenant reported blood dripping from his bathroom ceiling. Officers discovered four men in the apartment before making a gruesome discovery in the bathroom. There they found rubber gloves covered in blood on the floor, as well as a butcher knife, before seeing David's partially dismembered body in the tub. A hacksaw had been used to remove his arms and a leg.

The four Edmonton men pleaded guilty to being accessories after the fact to murder. They were handed prison sentences that ranged from thirty-two months to four-and-a-half years behind bars. Nobody has ever been charged with the actual killing of David Wong.

Edmonton's most notorious dismemberment killing occurred in July 1995, when the torso of Jo-Anne Dickson was found in a suitcase by the Groat Bridge. She had just left her common-law husband in Calgary and moved back to Edmonton with her two children, aged three and thirteen, in search of a better life.

One evening, Jo-Anne left the Commercial Hotel on Whyte Avenue with an unidentified man. Firefighters on a jet boat conducting training exercises later came across a suitcase on the banks of the North Saskatchewan River near Hawrelak Park. Inside was a black plastic garbage bag containing a woman's torso wrapped in a sheet. What happened to the rest of the body was a mystery.

Six months later, police received a tip about a twenty-seven-year-old *Star Trek* fan named Donald Smart, who made a confession to a friend on New Year's Day. He was arrested and charged with first-degree murder, along with offering an indignity to a dead body.

During an interview recorded at police headquarters, Smart told investigators that Jo-Anne was killed when she wouldn't have sex with him at his apartment. The pair had talked and fooled around a bit before Jo-Anne was stran-gled. To make sure she was dead, Smart dropped a barbell with about thirty-five kilograms of weight on her neck. He then dragged her body to the bathtub and poured bleach over it. Smart performed sexual acts on her body on sev-eral occasions, even while it was partially dismembered.

Using his bicycle, Smart took the suitcase with the torso to the river near the Groat Bridge. He carried the head and an arm in his backpack and dumped them at the Quesnell Bridge nearby. A medical examiner later testified it took Smart eight to ten hours to saw off Jo-Anne's arms, legs, and head with a sharp blade. Her body parts were dis-posed of during the course of a week.

Smart eventually led police to Jo-Anne's head, dropped in a twelve-metre-deep pipe embedded in a concrete sup-port pillar on the Quesnell Bridge. At another site, police recovered Jo-Anne's legs. Her arms were never found.

Smart was found guilty of second-degree murder and was handed a life sentence for murdering, sexually defil-ing, and dismembering Jo-Anne. Friends said Smart had a history of suicide attempts and self-abuse. At the time of his arrest, he worked at Rosie's Bar and Grill, three blocks from the Commercial Hotel.

It takes a certain type of individual to take the life of another human being, but criminologists say those who can dismember a dead body exist on a different level. Some simply do it to get rid of evidence. Others have a mental disorder or gain some kind of gratification from the act.

"The average person can't take a human body and start cutting it up," said Darryl Davies, a former parole officer and professor of criminology at Carleton University in Ottawa. "This has to be a person who has had this experi-ence in the past, doing it with animals or insects. When people read about [things like] this, it does cause a great deal of fear, because it's speaking to...what our species does to one another. These individuals [who do these things] symbolize very clearly and consistently something that is very ugly and disposable about our life."

GAIL MCCARTHY

The day Dianne Dawson received a phone call that her older sister living in Edmonton had suddenly disappeared is a day that's troubled her for forty-five years.

"I immediately started to cry," said Dianne about the call she received from her mother in November 1971. She was twenty years old, married, and pregnant at the time. Her father had left her mother that same year, leaving the family in turmoil.

"My fear was, she's gone. Mom said, 'Don't worry, they'll find her.' Deep down my worry was they [were] not going to find her," Dianne said.

Gail Eileen McCarthy was twenty-three years old and also pregnant when she vanished on November 14, 1971. She was on her way to work at the Misericordia Hospital, where she was employed as a medical technician. Wearing a brown coat with a white fur collar, white hospital stockings, brown imitation-seal-skin boots, and a Mexican hand-tooled leather purse, the petite woman with brown eyes and dirty blonde hair was last seen getting on a bus at around 6:30 a.m., but she never made it to work. Her husband of five months, Ian McCarthy, reported Gail missing eleven hours after she had left their basement apartment at 11820 124th Street to catch the bus a block away.

The couple had been visiting with friends the previous night. They sat around, talked, and watched television while Gail held the other couple's baby. The next morning, she woke up and kissed Ian goodbye, saying she'd see him in the afternoon.

"She'd always wake me up to kiss me goodbye. And if she had the day off, I'd kiss her goodbye when I was leaving," he said. "I was just about to leave to go scuba diving about 7:30 when the hospital phoned. They asked me if she was coming to work, and I said, 'Yes, but she may have missed the bus.' Usually if she missed the bus, she'd come home and wake me up to give her a ride. Then they phoned back at 8:30, and that really had me worrying."

An Edmonton bus driver later told Ian he picked up a woman matching Gail's description and dropped her off at a stop between 107th and 108th Avenue. It was the last time she was ever seen.

Originally from North Battleford, Saskatchewan, Gail moved to Edmonton about a year and a half before she disappeared. Her sisters remember her as a quiet, shy, and introverted person who loved poetry and baking.

The last time Dianne saw Gail was at her Edmonton apartment during a brief visit in September 1971. Gail was studying and cooking something on the stove and had some exciting news to share.

"She was so happy because she had just found out she was pregnant," said Dianne, adding, "Who walks off when they are three months pregnant and falls off the face of the Earth?"

Gail's disappearance left the family in disbelief, and as time passed by without any sign of her, they began to fear the worst. The family had suspicions that Ian was involved. He worked as a paratrooper for the military, said

Dianne, and bragged about how many ways he knew how to kill someone with his hands. Police, however, quickly ruled out Ian as a suspect.

About a month after Gail disappeared, Ian gave all her stuff away. According to Dianne, he drove the nearly six hours to North Battleford and left a suitcase with Gail's wedding dress outside her mother's house without saying a word to anybody. The luggage had been purchased for Gail as a graduation gift. Gail's younger sister, Lesley Richard, found the luggage sitting at the back door when she came home from a basketball practice. She was sixteen at the time.

Gail McCarthy on her wedding day. She was just twenty-three when last seen on November 14, 1971. She was on her way to work at the Misericordia Hospital in Edmonton when she disappeared. (Photo courtesy of Sun Media)

"We thought, 'Wow, this is great, she's home.' I have never seen such a look of disappointment when [my mother] saw that luggage and me," said Lesley.

In a desperate search for answers, the family made phone calls to various hospitals at around the time Gail was supposed to give birth to her child. They also went to a convent in Edmonton, since Gail was fairly spiritual and had once spoken about becoming a nun. But by the time spring rolled around, the reality of Gail's disappearance was starting to set in for Lesley.

"There were all those significant times—like when Dianne had her first child, and it's like, wow, she's not here to celebrate that," Lesley said.

As the years passed by, the family received snippets of information from different places and people, but nothing amounted to a significant lead. They even went to a medium, who said Gail was in the passenger side of a light blue car and was murdered, her body dumped somewhere in Edmonton near water and a zoo. Eventually, Dianne put her sister's disappearance in the back of her mind, but she phones her mother every year on Gail's birthday just to talk.

"I would never say why I was calling. When January third came it would be at the forefront," Dianne said.

With their father no longer alive, and the health of their elderly mother deteriorating, Lesley and Dianne hope to find closure soon. Until that day comes, the search for Gail will never end for the two sisters, and she remains in their memories.

"She's always there. I still think about her daily. There are some highlights during your life—when I had my son, when I got married—those kind of occasions that you kind of go, wow, there's somebody missing here," said an emotional Lesley from her home in Victoria, B.C. "You kind of hope that there will be closure. We don't believe that she is still alive. We think that she is gone. We are just hopeful that one day we can learn what happened to her."

"To think she was twenty-three years old. She didn't get to fulfill anything that she wanted to do," Dianne said. "It's just sad that nobody's been able to help her. She really hasn't had a voice. There's no closure. There's just nothing."

THE SOMALIS

The year 2011 came in with a bang. Three hours past midnight, shots erupted inside the Papyrus Restaurant and Lounge, an inner-city bar that was packed with patrons ringing in the new year. Mohamud Jama was among the celebrants.

Instead of making New Year's resolutions, the twenty-three-year-old was shot dead on the floor of the lobby while many people were still inside the bar. A second man, twenty-six, was taken to hospital with non-life-threatening injuries. Both men were known to police, who don't believe the shooting was random. A few days after the shooting, Mohamud was to have been sentenced on a charge of assault with a weapon for stabbing another man six times in the chest and abdomen in October 2007.

With so many witnesses to the shooting, Edmonton Homicide Staff Sergeant Bill Clark thought it should be an open-and-shut case. Instead, detectives were met with deafening silence—nobody wanted to talk.

"We are getting no cooperation from witnesses, and we believe they do know exactly who killed the guy. But none of them will say, which has been a problem when we run into these types of murders," said Bill, who was a detective at the time of the murder. Bill estimates at least a hundred people were inside the bar when the trigger was pulled. A few people have come forward, but only one person gave a description of the shooter.

"The investigation is going to go nowhere without cooperation," Bill added. "It's frustrating. We want to solve every murder we get. If we get cooperation, this one we could easily solve. There has to be at least a handful of people who know the shooter. The other guy won't talk either—the one who was shot. I think basically if they don't want to help, we should wrap these investigations up."

Bill's comments that day caused an uproar within Edmonton's Somali-Canadian community, forcing the police chief to issue an apology and mend fences with Somali leaders. But it wasn't the first time Bill had felt frustration with such cases, and it wasn't the first time Edmonton's Somali community had found themselves in mourning.

Since 2005 at least two dozen young Somali-Canadian men have died in Alberta—eleven of those in Edmonton between 2006 and 2009. With witnesses often hesitant to come forward, most of those cases remain unsolved, leaving detectives with few leads to follow.

Most of the murders are drug- or gang-related, and the victims are young men in their late teens or early twenties. They are children of a generation who fled war-torn Somalia two decades ago, seeking refuge from the brutal civil war sparked in 1991. After fleeing to neighbouring countries, many of them came to Toronto where they raised their children, often in poverty. Lured by the big bucks to be had in Alberta's booming oil patch, some of them ventured west with scores of other eastern Canadians who had dreams of becoming rich. But not everyone strikes gold.

Unemployed and struggling to make ends meet, some are pulled into the world of drugs and gangs that thrives in Edmonton's lucrative economy. High-level dealers can gross thousands of dollars a day selling crack and cocaine. It's an easy way to make a quick buck, but not everyone lives to escape the lifestyle.

Before the influx in Somali migration to Alberta, Vietnamese refugees came to the province in high numbers during the early 1990s. Violence also erupted among some of the Vietnamese gangs. On one occasion in July 2004, a brawl broke out between rival gangs attending two different wedding celebrations at a three-floor banquet hall and restaurant near Chinatown.

The dispute between guests from both weddings began near the second-floor staircase and spilled over to a landing area, where the body of twenty-four-year-old Tap Tran was found. When the violence ended, six people were injured, including the groom, who was stabbed in the throat. Tap was fatally stabbed in the neck. Minh Tang, twenty, was also stabbed and died more than a week later.

Four months later, Huy Le Nguyen died in a hail of bullets as he was standing outside a Vietnamese restaurant along Calgary Trail. A dark-coloured SUV drove up to the business. Someone inside the vehicle started shooting. Three people with the twenty-five-year-old were also wounded.

Police believe the shooting may have been retaliation for the deaths of Tap and Minh. Minh Nguyen's murder remains on the unsolved list, along with those of a number of other Edmonton gangsters.

By the time the violence among Vietnamese gangs calmed down, at least ten people had died over the course of five years. The violence picked up again later when other ethnic groups began clashing in the southeast Edmonton community of Mill Woods.

By 2009 Edmonton's Somali-Canadian community had reached a population of ten thousand people—the largest Somali-Canadian population outside of Ontario and the largest African-Canadian community in the city. By then, eight young Somali-Canadians had been gunned down. Most had links to the city's drug trade.

Local Somali leaders acknowledged there was a problem, that too many young men were being drawn to crime, but the leader pleaded with people not to paint everyone with the same brush. It wasn't until the shooting death of twenty-year-old Mohamed Khalif at Hermitage Park that same year that concerned parents and members of the community created a volunteer organization offering workshops and programs for families.

One community member explained that many parents work two jobs, so they don't have time to be at home with young people, who instead hang out with peers often involved in drugs or violence. Many of them fall behind in school due to a number of issues, including language barriers. They drop out and have no idea where to turn.

The ongoing gun violence had many members of the Somali-Canadian community on edge. Some accused police of turning a blind eye. At the time of Mohamud Jama's death, Mahamad Accord, president of the Alberta Somali Community, said community members wanted to cooperate with police, but were often scared to come forward for fear their lives would be at stake. Mahamad pointed a finger at Edmonton's mayor and council for not giving police the tools and resources needed to break down cultural barriers and ensure potential witnesses are protected. People want to cooperate, but Mahamad claimed witnesses had been intimidated and sometimes threatened for speaking out in the past. Bill Clark, however, said that was not the case.

"In thirty-five years of police work, I've never seen a witness hurt or hauled out and killed because they have said something to police. That's Hollywood stuff," he said. "If you're into gangs and you're a Hells Angels member, you might get dumped out, but that's your choice. You can take steps to get away from that. In the real world, people make threats all the time, but they never carry through."

Police have a good idea about who's responsible for the 2011 New Year's Eve slaying at Papyrus Restaurant and Lounge. Bill believes he knows Mohamud's killer, but he needs more evidence to lay charges. Detectives have spoken with the suspect during their investigation, but nobody has been willing to come forward and confirm he pulled the trigger. On one occasion, Bill and his partner flew to Ottawa to talk to a man who knows who shot Mohamud, but the pair were thrown out of the man's house within thirty minutes, closing another door on a hot lead.

"He's away from this life of crime, and he wouldn't talk to us. We know we have a witness here, we know this guy can give us the key piece to put someone in jail, bring a family some closure, and he won't do it," said Bill in 2014. "We can't force them to talk. That's not the way the law works. If that was your child, you would want that person to come forward. We will work on it, but once we get to the end of our last lead that's it, done. It's on the shelf until some new information comes up."

The relationship between Edmonton Police and the Somali-Canadian community has vastly improved in recent years. While distributing a picture of a thirty-year-old murder suspect, Bill praised the help detectives have received from the community, which assisted in solving the slaying of an eighteen-year-old man in March 2013.

Another case also came to a close with the help of the community. In April 2011, twenty-four-year-old Abdikadir Abdow was convicted of first-degree murder for the slaying of Mohamed Khalif and handed a life sentence with no chance of parole for twenty-five years. Mohamed and another man were held against their will at a north-side apartment before they were marched out to a car and driven to Hermitage Park, a popular place for dog walkers and families. They were ordered out of the vehicle. Abdow stood by them holding his rifle before turning and shooting Mohamed in the stomach, marking the city's fourth homicide in five days. Later in the day, two men, including Abdow, were taken into custody. Edmonton Police thanked members from the Somali-Canadian community for coming forward and providing them with information in relation to the case.

In a victim-impact statement entered during Abdow's sentencing hearing, Mohamed Khalif's older brother described the killing as a senseless and horrific crime. The Khalif family happily immigrated to Canada in 2003, following twelve years in a refugee camp in Kenya after fleeing war-torn Somalia. Their dream of living in Canada turned into a nightmare with the murder of their loved one.

"It haunts me to this day," wrote the brother in the statement, also addressing the killer.

"I want you to know that you by yourself have ruined my life. You took away my baby brother. I will never see him again because of you...I hope you will have to reflect about how your senseless act destroyed many lives."

WRONG PLACE, WRONG TIME

As a young man in Punjab, Dilbag Singh Sandhu always dreamed about some day immigrating to Canada. In 2003, that wish finally came true when he arrived in Alberta's capital city.

At first, Dilbag lived with his brothers as he adjusted to his foreign surroundings. Not wanting to be a burden, he eventually moved out on his own and worked two jobs to make ends meet. One of those jobs was at a Mac's convenience store located in a residential strip mall near 44th Street and 36th Avenue. When the twenty-nine-year-old wasn't working, he spent his time improving his English to ease the transition into Canadian life.

"He was a very shy guy. He wouldn't bother a soul. He was good with kids," said family friend Charan Saggu. Another friend described Dilbag as a very intelligent, educated, and religious man.

On the night of June 17, 2005, Dilbag's character traits didn't matter. Just before 1 a.m., two men in disguise burst into the Mac's convenience store, demanding money and cigarettes. One of them had a sawed-off shotgun.

Dilbag was one of two employees working that night and was sleeping in the back room when the masked men barged into the store. The frightened employee manning the front counter complied with the robber's orders. Dilbag came out of the back room as the thieves were heading for the door. One of the men fired a shot, hitting Dilbag in the abdomen.

At some point, one of the employees was able to set off a silent alarm to alert police that something was wrong at the store. When police arrived, they found Dilbag, who had only started working at the store two months earlier, dying from the gunshot wound. He went into cardiac arrest and died on the way to the hospital. The other clerk, who was sixty-three, was also rushed to hospital with stroke-like symptoms. The stress of the violence was too much for him to handle.

No customers were in the store at the time of the shooting, but a woman pulled up seconds after the fatal blast.

"I saw the man rolling around on the floor, covered in blood. He sat right up and then he fell over the other way," she said, adding she could see an older man behind the cash register.

"I don't know if he was pressing the panic button or what. He was almost lurching about. He looked like he was going to fall over. Then he just disappeared [behind the counter]."

Detective Brian Robertson had been in the homicide unit for three years at the time of the shooting. The case is one that made his head shake and still does to this day.

"He [Dilbag] didn't do anything to provoke them or cause them to shoot," said Brian. "It's absolutely an unnecessary, cold-blooded killing. He was a totally innocent victim. It was a robbery that was finished. There was no need to shoot him. It just makes no sense."

As news about the deadly shooting spread throughout the community the next day, a collection of flowers and stuffed toys surfaced outside the door of the convenience store, which was located across the street from an elementary school. Yellow police tape ran along the store front, and a crew had been in the night before to clean blood off the floor. A sign in the window stated there was no more than $50 in the store at night, adding to the anger many were already feeling over the senseless shooting.

Dilbag's grieving family was left trying to make sense of what happened. An estimated five hundred people gathered to remember the young man at his funeral. His mother flew in from India, a brother travelled from Los Angeles, and a sister came from Vancouver. Other relatives drove up from Calgary.

"This was a tragedy," said friend Bobby Gill. "It's a shock for the whole community. Even, I would say, for the whole city."

Three months after the deadly shooting, police announced a $40,000 reward for information leading to an arrest. They also released parts of the store's video footage from the night of the murder in an effort to generate more clues.

The case continued to attract interest from the public, many of whom were shaken for months by such random violence. The convenience store was a frequent stop on the way home from work for many residents. Now fear had crept into their community.

Dilbag's family hoped the killer would be caught quickly, but two years later, the case remained unsolved. Six months after the slaying, Dilbag's mother passed away, marking another sad chapter in the story.

"The family is sad," said Dilbag's older brother during a community barbecue to mark the second anniversary of the unsolved homicide. "The family is not feeling very good, because the police could not find the killer."

Meanwhile, many residents were still thinking about what they could do to help police solve the murder.

Early on, police identified and investigated some theories that continue to be worked on, with hopes of finding the killer. As more time passes, Brian Robinson hopes the shooter's accomplice or someone else will have the courage to step forward and give police that key piece of information to move the case forward.

"I think we've got some really good evidence. It's just a matter of [needing] that one good piece," he said in 2014. "There's a lot of cases that are just one phone call away from getting on to the right people or getting stronger on the people you're already looking at. We've done a lot of work on this file over the years. I wouldn't suggest that we're close, but we've laid enough groundwork that if we get that right piece of information, we'll be off to the races on it."

Dilbag's murder was a case of being in the wrong place at the wrong time. It's the same story for Erin Anne Tilley.

Like many Canadians living on the east coast, the twenty-seven-year-old Newfoundlander had moved to the West right after high school, in search of better opportunities. She soon found work as a personal banker at a car

Dilbag Singh Sandhu. He was working at an Edmonton convenience store in June 2005 when he was fatally shot during a robbery. (Photo courtesy of Sun Media)

dealership in Edmonton. She wanted to be closer to her older sister, Jodi, who was already living in the city. Another sibling soon followed, along with their parents.

"St. John's is a great place to live, but it's hard to find jobs," said Erin in an interview with an Edmonton newspaper for an article on population shift within Canada. "It was a nice change of pace. I'm working now and going to school. I love it here. It's booming. There's an awful lot of people here from outside the province. Everyone knows there's opportunity."

In December 2007, Erin left the Empire Ballroom nightclub at West Edmonton Mall in the early morning hours. She was with a group of people, some of whom she had just met for the first time. She got into a vehicle with three of them and drove to a gas station shortly after leaving the club.

While the vehicle was stopped at an intersection in west Edmonton, another car pulled up beside it. Someone in the car fired several shots at the vehicle Erin was in, striking her in the head, neck, and upper chest. She was taken to hospital, but was pronounced dead on arrival. The woman who drove Erin there refused to cooperate with police.

At around 2:45 a.m. that morning, a witness phoned 911 to report shots fired, possibly between a blue car and a white car at the intersection of 95th Avenue and 156th Street. Police believe others were in the car with Erin and wanted them to come forward, along with someone pumping gas at the nearby Petro Canada station. Investigators also appealed to the people inside a third vehicle which was stopped at the intersection, although they didn't believe anyone in that car was involved in the gunfire.

As the investigation progressed, police neither believed Erin was the intended target nor that she was directly involved with any gangs. Officers had not been familiar with her name until her death. Friends said she was in the wrong place at the wrong time, perhaps caught up with the wrong crowd.

"She wasn't troubled. Her family was everything to her. She was beautiful...inside and out. Now she's looking down on us from up there," said Melissa Tizzard, one of Erin's friends from Newfoundland. "All heads turned when she walked into a room. She walked into a room and just lit it up. She was always happy, always wanted to do everything for everyone else. She was just a good person."

Scott Hammond, Erin's high-school sweetheart, regularly kept in touch with her throughout the years. When Erin went back to Newfoundland for a visit, she told Scott how good her life was in Edmonton.

"I remember her saying that she was very happy that she chose to live in Edmonton, which I find a little ironic now," Scott said. "She was just as full of life as I can remember. She was the life of the party. You were just a better person for knowing her."

Erin's sister agreed. In her eulogy at the funeral, she described Erin as a lover of animals, debating, golf, and above all, family and friends. "Everyone who came into contact with her adored her," she said.

A year after Erin's death, police had a few more answers, but who pulled the trigger remained a mystery. They believe the man sitting beside Erin in the back seat of the car may have been the intended target, but none of the three men who were in the vehicle will cooperate with the investigation.

Homicide detectives believe an incident inside the Empire Ballroom could have initiated the shooting, and they suspect the people involved in the beef at the bar followed the car Erin was in. What exactly happened next is anybody's guess until witnesses to the murder are willing to confess the secrets they've been hiding for years.

BRENDA MCCLENAGHAN

I f Brenda McClenaghan was going to stay out late, she always phoned her parents to let them know where she was. So when silence followed in the days after the twenty-year-old went out for an evening of drinking and dancing with some friends, her parents began to fear their youngest daughter had been abducted.

"We feel someone's got her. She just doesn't do this kind of thing," said her father, Robert McClenaghan.

Her two friends last saw Brenda when they left the Pink Panther Lounge at the Convention Inn on the night of Saturday, January 11, 1986. The south-side lounge was a favourite spot for the hairdressing student to hang out with her friends, but as the night wound down, Brenda wasn't quite ready to go home. While her friends left in a cab, she stuck around a while longer, planning to drive her own car back to her Mill Woods home.

"She was having a good time. Brenda was in a good mood," said Paul Pridham, who danced with Brenda at the lounge. He saw her leave alone just after last call.

"She said to me, 'I'm tired, I think I'll go home.' She was smiling. Everything seemed okay."

Brenda left the hotel and walked to her 1975 blue four-door Chevrolet Impala at around 1:30 a.m. It was the last time anyone would see the pretty, five-foot-nine brunette with long hair and green eyes alive.

Robert and his wife came back to Edmonton Sunday, after spending the weekend at the log cabin they were building at Baptiste Lake, 157 kilometres north of the city. Upon their return, one of Brenda's friends called to say she could not be reached. The McClenaghans wasted no time in contacting police.

A distraught Robert spent Monday scouring city parking lots and hotels for any trace of his daughter, who had moved back to her parents' home three months prior, after breaking up with her fiancé.

The next day, a city homicide detective told the worried couple that Brenda's car was found locked and empty in a parking lot at Northtown Mall. The car was now being combed for clues, but police found no sign of a struggle or forced entry. The wheel wells, however, were clotted with mud and bits of grass, indicating the vehicle may have been driven through a rural area. Gripped with worry, the McClenaghans issued a public plea for Brenda to call home.

"It's terrible, all the things that go through your mind at a time like this. All we can do now is wait by the phone and pray for something to happen," said Robert. "You always hope, but you have to be realistic about these things."

With Brenda's name and picture plastered across the news, offers of assistance began pouring from the public into police headquarters, and the citizens of Edmonton began to mobilize. About thirty members of the Enoch Indian Reserve (Enoch Cree Nation) scoured the bush on land just west of Winterburn. Esso Petroleum had workers search nearby fields. The Convention Inn, where Brenda spent her last night, put up a $1,000 reward for information leading to her whereabouts. Another $8,000 was thrown into the pot, including $2,500 raised by fellow hairstyling students during a cut-a-thon.

Mounties also joined in the search, using an RCMP helicopter with an infrared scanner to scour rural areas. By now, city police had searched about 75 per cent of Edmonton and were receiving hundreds of tips each day, but Brenda was still nowhere to be found.

On the night she disappeared, Brenda was wearing a two-tone blue jean jacket with a zipper, blue jeans, a black shirt and sweater, and black high-heeled shoes. As the investigation progressed, police revealed that the young woman's jeans, turned inside out, were found inside her car. Her shoes and several cassette tapes were also missing.

Police also revealed another chilling detail—a woman was chased by a man near the Convention Inn only two days after Brenda disappeared. The man grabbed the woman's blouse, but she was able to escape and hide behind a dumpster.

Nearly two weeks after Brenda's bizarre disappearance, Barry Fox was walking his black, six-year-old Labrador retriever, Dee, on his quiet, secluded south-side acreage near 76th Avenue and 18th Street. He threw a piece of rubber down the laneway. Dee brought it back the first time, but after that she didn't want to play.

In order to get her to exercise, Barry walked down the laneway with Dee trotting beside him. That's when he remembered the orange colour he had seen in the trees four days earlier as he drove into his driveway.

Barry decided to walk into the trees to investigate. He saw an orange cord along with what he thought was some kind of foot, possibly an animal's. His initial thought was that someone had poached a deer, since a lot of small game lived in the area. Then he walked closer.

"As I got close I could see the other leg," said Barry, who then noticed some hair that looked like a woman's cheap wig. "I thought it might have been a mannequin."

Three metres from the tree, Barry was struck with horror when he realized that what he was seeing was the body of a young woman. She had been strangled with a piece of wire and tied to a tree with the orange extension cord. The woman was half-naked and face down, only her legs and part of her head visible through the snow.

Police hadn't told the public about the orange extension cord they knew was missing from Brenda's car. Barry believes revealing that detail could have saved a day or week of personal anguish for the McClenaghan family. When police earlier asked property owners to check their land, Barry had gone for a walk with Dee, but he concentrated mainly on the back of the property, looking for tire tracks as officers had requested.

After the chilling discovery, about twenty-five police staff, including homicide detectives, identification members, patrol officers, and task-force members descended upon the area, setting up a mobile command post and filming the scene. Police took fingerprints off everything they could and combed the area for evidence, but a fresh coat of snow left no footprints around the body. Investigators later hauled four bags of evidence from the grisly crime scene. Two of the bags appeared to contain snow, while the others had foliage and tree branches. An autopsy later revealed the young woman had also been raped.

As speculation began to grow that the woman found in the woods was Brenda, the McClenaghans braced themselves for the worst. Instead of celebrating his daughter's twenty-first birthday, Robert identified her body as the one found tied to a tree in the wooded area on the city's south side. He took one look at his daughter's remains, then turned away. It was the hardest thing he's ever had to do.

"It's a relief that at least we know where she is now. We know where she is and we can begin to try and live with it. Not knowing is what really hurt us. At least we have her back," said Robert, adding that the strain of the previous two weeks had taken a toll on the family. "We're tired. It's not the end of the road yet. We've still got a long way to go."

Brenda's death caused more public concern than any other crime in Edmonton at the time and seemed to put everyone on edge. Worried women and parents across the city turned to martial arts and self-defence classes to protect themselves and their children. City gun stores also noticed an increased number of women seeking firearms.

A few days after Brenda's frozen body was discovered, around three hundred concerned citizens stood in the cold in Sir Winston Churchill Square to express their sympathy in an emotional candlelight vigil. Bundled in scarves and toques, men, women, and children held candles, sang songs, and shed their tears and anger. The vigil was organized by the Alberta Status of Women Action Committee and the Sexual Assault Centre of Edmonton.

As the search continued for Brenda's killer, prominent citizens, such as Premier Don Getty, offered rewards for his capture. A $13,000 bounty was raised to make an arrest in the case. A six-hour Crime Stoppers telethon broadcast attracted another $47,424 in pledges.

In order to advance the investigation, city police asked the U.S. Federal Bureau of Investigation (FBI) to prepare a psychological profile of the killer. Police also hoped a Crime Stoppers segment would jog someone's memory and provide fresh clues.

The night Brenda disappeared from the Pink Panther Lounge, William (Bill) Roy Tame, along with a couple of his friends, had been in the bar, sitting across the room from Brenda and her friends, near the door. The three men from Brandon, Manitoba, had arrived in Edmonton early that morning along with Tame's brother, Reg Tame, who came to the city to purchase a 1975 Chevy. Earlier that day, all seemed well as the Tame brothers inspected the Chevy together. The pair shared a passion for tinkering with old cars.

The four men booked a room at the Relax Inn, just north of the Convention Inn, and spent a typical tourist day at West Edmonton Mall and the slot-car races. Reg went to visit his in-laws that evening. The other three men decided to head out for a night on the town.

The trio began the night at the Terrace Inn, then made their way to the Pink Panther at around 9 p.m. Two of the men drank heavily, but Tame sipped from two coolers over the course of the entire evening.

The three men later parted ways, when two of them went to the hotel room of a woman they had met earlier in the evening. Tame was supposedly heading back to the Relax Inn. Instead, he met an unsuspecting Brenda in the parking lot outside the Convention Inn and pounced on her as she opened her car door.

Shoving her across to the passenger seat, Tame took the wheel and left the parking lot, heading off for a dark spot to commit his dark deeds. He parked in an industrial area, then raped the young woman in the front seat of her car before heading outside of the city to further assault and then kill his victim. Reg was afraid his brother had been up to no good when he stumbled into their hotel room at around 8 a.m.

"He looked like he had a bad night," Reg said. "He looked like he hadn't had much sleep. I asked him if he'd gotten into any trouble or anything, and he replied, 'No.'"

Tame later told his brother more about the events that night, stating he was with a girl. Reg asked if he had cheated on his wife, to which his brother replied, "Not really," stating he only had oral sex with the girl. It wasn't until Reg received a letter in the mail from Edmonton Police on the morning of February 14 that he heard the real story of what happened that night. The letter described Brenda's brutal slaying and asked for information. The only reason Reg received the letter was because the four Brandon men had stayed in a hotel near the Convention Inn. It was one of up to four thousand letters police had mailed to people registered in Edmonton hotels the night Brenda went missing.

Reg's heart was broken when he handed the letter to his brother and asked, "You didn't have anything to do with this, did you?"

"Yes," Tame replied. Reg didn't know what to do, so the pair went for a drive.

"He said, 'One thing I want you to know, it's not the Bill you know that did this,'" said Reg. "The first thing he wanted to do was kill himself, but I told him to think a little further than that because he had a family to think about."

Tame was silent for a few minutes when Reg asked if he was sorry about the brutal killing. Eventually he said he was sorry for his wife and son, but added that the "Bill" who did it wasn't sorry and didn't want to talk about it. Reg suggested his brother sign himself in at the local mental hospital, but Tame decided to talk first with his psychology teacher at Brandon University, where he was taking first-year science courses. Eventually he called a lawyer.

The thirty-four-year-old finally went to Brandon police and was charged with first-degree murder. He underwent a thirty-day psychiatric examination and assessment at

Alberta Hospital in Edmonton and was confirmed to be a psychopath, but legally sane.

News of the arrest came as a relief for the McClenaghan family, who hoped women living in Edmonton could now walk the streets again without fear. Those who knew Bill Tame were in complete shock. Nobody could believe the mild-mannered car nut could be capable of such a vicious crime.

Described as a nice, quiet man who enjoyed nothing more than souping up old cars, Tame was an unemployed welder who had a two-year-old son with his wife. He was going to university and reportedly doing well. Neighbours in his apartment building couldn't believe the charges.

"It doesn't seem real," said one woman, who didn't want to be named. She described herself as a close friend of Tame, who went to his place for weekly dinners and movies. "He's the kind of person you could get advice from and look up to."

Tame, however, had a dark side. At the age of nineteen, he began serving ten years in jail for the brutal rape of a fifteen-year-old girl in Brandon. The teen was home alone when she heard a noise at the back door. She suddenly saw Tame, nude from the waist down, standing beside her bed.

Tame jumped on the teen's bed and forced her into having sex. She managed to flee into a basement bedroom and lock the door, but Tame broke it down, attacking the terrified teen sexually with a beer bottle before having sex with her again. A day into the trial, Tame pleaded guilty to one count of rape. Reports also stated he was a former glue sniffer and had dabbled in prostitution.

Edmonton Police arrested Tame for Brenda's murder moments after he told detectives something only the killer would know. In a tape-recorded interview with city

Homicide Detective Mike Strulick, Tame admitted to using motor oil as a sexual lubricant the night Brenda was killed. It was one of the handful of facts police had held back from the public. The confession proved to be vital to the investigation, since no physical evidence was ever found linking him to the crime.

Inspector Brian Scott, the man who headed the Edmonton Police investigation, was thankful and relieved when he learned about the arrest. Although the case was complex, there was never a time when investigators became discouraged, due to the thousands of leads rolling in from across the country. The Crime Stoppers tip lines were constantly busy, and a special phone line, crewed around the clock, was installed at police headquarters to deal with the large number of calls from citizens. Some investigators worked sixteen hours a day from the start, while others logged hundreds of hours trying to solve the case before they finally got the big break.

In October 1986, after pleading guilty to his crime, Tame was sentenced to life in prison with no chance of parole for twenty-five years. The court heard that Brenda was stripped from the waist down and forced to walk into the woods through the snow in bare feet. Her hands were bound together behind her back and around a tree before she was sexually assaulted. A nylon stocking was looped around her neck, along with some stereo speaker wires from her car. A chunk of wood was twisted in place underneath the copper wiring. Turning the wood literally squeezed the life and breath out of the young woman.

Tame told the judge he was sorry for all the grief caused by his actions. He also apologized to Brenda's shaken parents.

"I'd like to take this opportunity to express my deepest regret to Mr. and Mrs. McClenaghan. Saying I'm sorry does not even begin to express the remorse I feel for the loss and grief I've caused," said Tame, as tears streamed down the face of Brenda's mother, seated in the front row of the courtroom. "I also regret the grief I've caused my family," he added.

Outside of court, Brenda's father rejected Tame's words as opportunism. "I would like to make myself look sweet in front of a judge, too, if I was up for twenty-five years," he said. "We all apologize in our life, but a lot of times we don't mean it. There isn't an apology in the world that's going to bring back anything."

HERE TODAY, GONE TOMORROW

One night in the spring of 1992, Adolph Gurnick tipped back a few drinks and decided to walk back to the friend's house he'd been staying at in north Edmonton. Instead of arriving safely at the home, the fifty-two-year-old was found lying in a back alley at 12943 122nd Street in the Calder neighbourhood. An autopsy revealed that he had been beaten on the right side of his head and suffered numerous stab wounds to the chest. Police believe it was a robbery gone wrong. The case has now been cold for more than twenty years.

The pain still runs deep for the remaining members of Adolph's family. His brother, Edward Gurnick, still harbours much hurt and anger. He's lost for words about the murder and finds it difficult to talk about. Adolph's sister-in-law, Leslie Gurnick, was in disbelief the day she received the phone call from police delivering the grim news and continues to wonder why someone would viciously take the life of such a generous and kind man.

"He would have given anybody anything. That's why it's so painful because he would have given them the money if they had asked for it," said Leslie. "He was very generous and he was very kind."

According to Leslie, Adolph lived in the hamlet of Violet Grove near the town of Drayton Valley, southwest of Edmonton. He was in the city visiting a friend and possibly looking for employment, when his life came to a sudden end.

Staff Sergeant Bill Clark of the Edmonton Police homicide unit was working for forensic identification services at the time of Adolph's slaying. Bill said there were signs of a fight, and there could have been more than one attacker, based on Adolph's injuries. He believes the violent attack was a crime of opportunity.

"They may have followed him from the Dover [hotel] and just decided to rob him. He was just an old man walking in the neighbourhood harmlessly, not bothering anyone," said Bill. "I don't think the investigation will ever truly be solved. It's just one of those senseless acts the community should be outraged at."

When Yvonne Thorn wakes up every morning, she sees the baby boy she never got a chance to know. A picture of Robin Thorn hangs on the wall of her bedroom. It's one of the only memories she has left of her eleven-month-old baby before his life came to a violent end.

"I look at his picture every day," said Yvonne, from her home in Saskatchewan. She still has difficulty explaining to others what happened to the smiling baby boy on the wall. "[My granddaughter] wonders who that is, but it's kind of hard to explain to her. I don't tell her the details."

It was around 11:40 a.m. on June 27, 1997, when Robin's tiny, lifeless body was discovered in the bedroom of his Norwood home at 11406 97th Street in Edmonton. Yvonne found the baby lying on two bare mattresses on the floor when she returned after a night away from home. He was covered in blood, wearing nothing but a diaper. Police said the cause of death was numerous puncture wounds to the abdomen and chest.

The night before Robin was slain, a party was going on in the garage Yvonne shared with her common-law husband, who was supposed to be watching the baby, along with his three older siblings.

Yvonne has suspicions about who's responsible for the killing. She claims a man who was at her house the night of the party had threatened to harm her the night before. That man, however, has since passed away.

Yvonne never dreamed that fourteen years would pass and her son's killer would still be roaming free. She feels someone should pay for the crime so that she and her family can feel what it's like to have closure instead of wondering who took the life of the smiling baby boy.

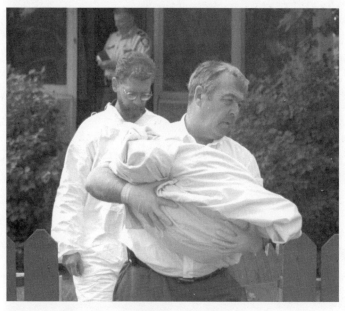

The body of eleven-month-old Robin Thorn is removed from a house in June 1997. Robin was found with numerous puncture wounds to the abdomen and chest inside the home. (Photo by Dale MacMillan / Courtesy of Sun Media)

"Someone should have been held accountable," said Yvonne, who packed her bags shortly after Robin's death and moved her family to the One Arrow Reserve near Domremy, Saskatchewan, in order to be closer to loved ones. Her common-law husband has since passed away.

"My other kids took it kind of hard as they grew up. They knew something happened. I didn't want to be around the city after that," she said.

As the years pass by, Yvonne tries to focus on the good memories she has of her fourth and youngest child, who she described as a good-natured boy who loved to smile. One of her fondest memories is of a smiling Robin, lying on his back, moving his legs, arms, and head whenever she said, "Let's see my baby wiggle."

"It's good to talk about it once in a while," said Yvonne. "It's about who he was, not about what happened."

DYLAN MCGILLIS

A s the hearts of some families continue to be pained by the unsolved murders of their loved ones, others have found closure after several painful years of waiting for justice to be served. The McGillises are among those who had hoped and prayed for that day to come, yet were shocked and emotional when it finally did.

On November 19, 2006, Dylan Cole McGillis was out celebrating the beginning of an exciting new chapter in his life. The twenty-year-old and his girlfriend, who was going to school in Edmonton, had recently found out they were expecting a baby. Dylan was in the city making arrangements to move from the small Saskatchewan–Alberta border city of Lloydminster to Edmonton to be with his girlfriend. Then tragedy struck.

Packed with numerous bars and lively restaurants, Edmonton's Whyte Avenue was hopping with party-goers letting loose on a Saturday night. Dylan and his friends were among the rowdy crowds. At around 2:30 a.m., they were leaving a club near 106th Street, when Dylan was approached by a group of males with whom he exchanged words.

Dylan and his friends walked away from the verbal exchange, but the group—which quickly swelled from about five to well over fifteen people—chased after Dylan and assaulted him. Dylan managed to get up from the ground and was guided away by one of his friends, but the people in the group continued to pursue him and the others.

One of the people in the group stepped forward, pulled a knife, and stabbed Dylan twice in the abdomen. He died later that day from his injuries, marking the city's thirty-fourth homicide of 2006.

One of Dylan's friends, a pregnant woman, threw her body on him during the altercation in an effort to protect him from his attackers. She suffered cuts to her arms, but otherwise escaped physically unharmed. Another man was pulled from his truck nearby and assaulted just minutes after the fatal stabbing. Police believe it was the same group of attackers in both incidents.

"We're not dealing with someone who lost his temper. We're dealing with cowards and thugs," said Ernie Schreiber, an Edmonton Police homicide detective at the time of the murder.

Surrounded by grieving relatives, Dylan's parents issued an emotional plea for anyone who witnessed their son's death to come forward to police.

"There were 13,000 people out on these streets [the night Dylan was killed]," said Dylan's mother, Marlene McGillis, in 2009, choking back tears during the annual vigil they held for their son. But as more time passed by, and no one came forward, family members were thrown deeper into an ocean of grief. All they could do was wait for a break in the case, and to continue holding the yearly vigil until that happened.

"I'm angry no one has been charged with Dylan's murder yet," said his father, Grant McGillis, at the same vigil in 2009.

Two more years passed before the family finally heard the news they were desperately waiting for—a twenty-four-year-old Edmonton man named Cleophas (Cliff) Decoine-Zuniga had been arrested and charged with one count of manslaughter. Police also released information about a person they hoped to identify—an Asian man, approximately five foot two to five foot five, slender with dark hair.

News that a suspect had finally been charged came as a shock to Grant. He knew police were continuing to investigate Dylan's death, but he had not heard any details about whether or not they were even close to an arrest. The news threw him into a wave of emotions after years of frustration, knowing his son was murdered for no reason

"It brings all the bad memories back, right in the forefront of your life again," said Grant. "My head is kind of spinning in twenty different directions. It's been a long time. That's one thing I always feared—that somebody could get away with this and go unpunished for such a horrific crime."

On Father's Day that year, Dylan's daughter, then three, took a card to his gravesite to remember the father she never had a chance to meet. And since his death, family get-togethers have never been the same. Every holiday is a painful reminder that someone's not there. "It's a really sad thing that never goes away," Grant said.

By the time October 2013 rolled around, friends and family—wearing T-shirts with Dylan's picture on them—were applauding, after a Court of Queen's Bench judge found Decoine-Zuniga guilty for his role in Dylan's death.

The judge told the courtroom that he was convicting Decoine-Zuniga, who was not the stabber, of being a party to manslaughter as a result of him being an "aider and abettor." He was a part of the group that had the common intention of carrying out unlawful acts—including inflicting the beating on Dylan's group, the judge added.

"He participated in the violence by punching and kicking Mr. McGillis and stomping on him with his foot," said the judge, noting the accused also pursued Dylan as he attempted to escape the attack.

Police had targeted Decoine-Zuniga in a "Mr. Big" sting operation in 2011, which involved undercover officers posing as members of a fictitious criminal organization in order to get him to reveal his involvement in the slaying. In three separate recorded admissions, Decoine-Zuniga confessed to being involved in the swarming, punching Dylan as he was being stabbed, then kicking and stomping on his head before fleeing the scene.

Dylan McGillis's parents, Grant and Marlene, hold photos of their slain son outside of Court of Queen's Bench after reading victim-impact statements. (Photo by Ian Kucerak / Courtesy of Sun Media)

Ernie was the primary investigator on the case and noted that the biggest challenge for police was that witnesses were identifying different people as the one responsible for stabbing Dylan.

"We had a really good idea about who was responsible. [But] in a case like that, you just have to be patient," said Ernie. "That was a case that reached a dead end, but then in time more evidence came forward...At the end of the day the truth has come out, and that's what we all strive for," Ernie added.

In March 2014, Decoine-Zuniga was sentenced to five years in prison for his role in Dylan's death. Grant said that even a hundred-year sentence wouldn't have been enough for the damage that's been done. Both he and his now ex-wife are hopeful the actual killer will be caught as the investigation continues.

During the sentencing hearing, Decoine-Zuniga read a prepared statement in which he apologized to Dylan's family, who shed many tears as they read their victim-impact statements before the court.

"She never met her father," said Marlene, speaking of her granddaughter. "You've taken her father away from her." The grief-stricken mother also spoke of her own wounded soul and the dark hole left in her heart from the loss of her son, whom she described as a unique young man with a truly kind heart.

"Dylan will always live on, because I carry his heart within my heart, and you, Decoine-Zuniga, will never be able to hurt us again because you are not worth my time."

LIANA WHITE

On the outside, everything appeared normal between Michael White and his wife, Liana. The young married couple was preparing to welcome their second child into the Warwick Crescent home they'd been living in for four years with their three-year-old daughter, Ashley. White appeared to be thrilled about the addition to their growing family.

A former military man, White now worked as a heavy-duty mechanic, while Liana was employed as a clerk in the neo-natal intensive care unit at Royal Alexandra Hospital. The pair met in 1998 at Esmeralda's Night Club, not long after Liana moved to Edmonton from Kelowna. They married two years later, becoming the proud parents of a daughter the following year. Liana was White's soul-mate—a woman who always put others first.

When the twenty-nine-year-old mother failed to show up for work on the morning of July 12, 2005, friends and family began to worry. White told police he hadn't seen his wife since 6:15 a.m., when she had left the house. That same morning, police received a call about a suspicious vehicle parked in a lot next to a soccer field at 157th Avenue and 116th Street—a five-minute drive from the couple's home. Several witnesses reported seeing the SUV in the lot before 6:15 a.m.

At the parking lot, officers found Liana's brown Ford Explorer with the door wide open and the keys still inside. Her purse was outside, and her wallet was missing. Credit cards, a health care card, cell phone, and other ID were strewn on the ground. A pair of Liana's shoes was next to the vehicle.

"This is scary," said Inspector Jamie Ewatski the day after Liana's vehicle was found. "We all think about Punky Gustavson [see pages 52–57]. These things are out of the ordinary."

On the second day his wife was missing, White choked back tears as he spoke to reporters in front of the couple's home, pleading for her safe return. He took a moment to compose himself before urging Liana to stay strong, then he retreated back inside the bungalow without answering any questions.

"My wife is a good person, never hurt anybody, never would," he told a television news station. "She would never hurt a fly. She is a gentle person."

Police expanded their search to include areas beyond the scene where Liana's vehicle was found. Soon search-and-rescue crews became involved, combing the fields near the couple's Castle Downs home for any signs of the missing woman, who was

Michael White, outside his north-end Edmonton home, during an interview with reporters. White was later found responsible for his wife's death. (Photo courtesy of Sun Media)

then four months pregnant. Residents were asked to search their yards and check if anything seemed out of place. Homicide detectives also interviewed White, but they did not consider him a suspect. Police also launched an intense search of the White's single-storey home, asking him to leave for the duration of their investigation.

"They can't make a mistake," said White, while he was staying with his in-laws. "They have to cover their tails and every angle possible. Am I upset about it? Sure, but I have to support them. So we'll sit back and be relocated as much as possible so they can do their job. They can eliminate that and go a different route."

The thought that police might somehow link him to the disappearance had occurred to White during the search of his home, but he said he and those who surrounded him with love knew the truth. As White waited for news about his missing wife, he spent his days organizing searches of fields and parks for any sign of where she might be. The worried husband forced himself to stay composed for the sake of his daughter, who by now was beginning to understand something was terribly wrong.

But White couldn't help but fear the worst. On the afternoon of July 17, those fears became a reality when a volunteer search team organized by White found an unidentified body on the side of a country road near a Sturgeon County subdivision. The remote area surrounded by canola fields was less than a five-minute drive from St. Albert city limits and not far from the couple's home. The next day, White was charged with second-degree murder and offering an indignity to a body.

"It's a nightmare you can't wake up from. I still don't believe it's happened," said a neighbour after hearing about the arrest. "They were regular suburban people, like a normal family. They mowed their own lawn and had barbecues and worked on their house and helped other neighbours. Normal people, like all of us. His big joy in life was being a husband and father. Something has gone horribly wrong."

Police held off confirming the identity of the woman's body found by White's own search party, but the search for Liana was suddenly suspended. An autopsy later revealed that the decomposing body found face down in the ditch was indeed the woman they had been looking for. Her bra was placed above her head and her panties pulled down. None of her other clothing was found.

Liana had two stab wounds to the back area and cuts on her hand consistent with defence wounds from a struggle. The exact fatal wound could not be identified due to the body decomposition, but the medical examiner believed it was likely in the neck region or from manual strangulation.

Throughout the week of searching for Liana, investigators allowed White to make public pleas for her safe return as a strategy to see what he would do. Some of the evidence found earlier in the investigation had changed their focus to White as the killer, and they placed him on round-the-clock surveillance. During two searches of the couple's home, officers uncovered 150 pieces of evidence.

News of Liana's murder and of White being the accused killer was devastating for the couple's families, but the most devastated of all was their three-year-old daughter, who was now in the care of her grandmother.

"She's lost both her mom and dad," said Detective Michael Campeau, speaking of the arrest. "It's not a victory for the police service. It's a tragic day for two families. We're not here to celebrate anything."

Two months after White's arrest, a heartbroken mother, Maureen Kelly, stood in front of a wooden cross that marked the place where Liana's decomposing body was found. Maureen went to the cross from time to time to make sure it hadn't been disturbed. Tufts of her daughter's long dark hair were still visible among the broken branches, some of which were used to cover the body.

"It was a brutal murder. It bothers me to think she must have been so scared. To have this happen to her is outrageous...I miss her so much. I miss her phone calls. I miss seeing her. My heart's broken," said Maureen, who was terrified the day White called to say Liana was missing.

That terror turned to shock when her son-in-law was pegged as the man responsible for ending her daughter's life, but Maureen was forced to pick up the pieces and carry on, caring for the couple's child.

"I have a child to care for now. I have to continue caring for her. And I want to do it," she said. "She's my focal point now. Poor little girl. One day she has a mother and a father and a home, and the next day Mom's dead, Dad's in jail. Her world's been turned upside down."

Those who knew Liana also felt like their world had been turned upside down. Some two hundred people lit candles and walked from a downtown bar to a nearby park, where they signed a guestbook and remembered their beloved friend. Organizers not only wanted to raise funds for the education and future care of Ashley but also to draw attention to the issue of domestic violence.

"This made a victim of all of us, without having been hit and talked down to," said Pam Duncan, who had worked with Liana at the hospital.

"She was a co-worker, and a friend, and a lot of people loved her," another former colleague said.

Before his trial even began, court documents revealed some damaging evidence against White. At around 5 a.m. on the day Liana's Ford Explorer was found, the vehicle was recorded on a video security camera at Richard's Pub going from the direction of the White home to the parking lot where it was abandoned. Twelve minutes later, the video shows a man matching White's description running from the playground area back toward the nearby White home.

Police not only noted the items strewn around Liana's vehicle at the scene but also the placement of the driver's seat and the interior rear-view mirror, which were adjusted to fit a person of White's size as opposed to that of his significantly smaller wife.

Two days after Liana disappeared, police saw White late in the evening in a grassy field between his home and the spot where the body was later found. He picked up two garbage bags and returned them to his vehicle, bringing them home. Later that night, police watched White put the bags out for garbage pickup the next morning. The bags were seized after an officer rode along with a garbage truck.

Inside the two black bags, police found wet bloody paper towels, gloves, two bloody sponges, a broken lamp that matched a lamp found in the couple's bedroom, and bloody clothing identified by White as belonging to him. DNA testing of blood found on some of the items showed it also belonged to Liana. Blood was also found in various locations of the couple's bedroom and in the back of the Explorer.

On the first day of White's much anticipated, month-long murder trial in November 2006, the soft-spoken man wearing a black suit jacket stood up in the prisoner's box and quietly stated, "I am not guilty." It was a statement that would be echoed throughout the course of the trial, despite the evidence the Crown had against him.

The Crown claimed that White killed Liana in their home, dragged her body into the garage, put it into her SUV, then dumped her remains in a ditch. He tossed evidence from the killing into the garbage bags that he left in the grassy field, only to return later and pick them up, unwittingly under police surveillance. The SUV was left in a parking lot and staged to look like a robbery in an effort to cover up his crime.

The jury heard that experts found DNA belonging to both Michael and Liana on two latex gloves and a sock in the garbage bags collected by police from the couple's home. One of the gloves was found in the right front pocket of a pair of bloodstained pants inside the bags, while the second was from a first-aid kit also found inside the bags.

Police also discovered evidence of a cleanup in the bedroom, where traces of blood were found on a baseboard by the nightstand, the nightstand, a bedding skirt, a wall, the floor, and a baseboard beside the bed. It was consistent with a stabbing-type attack on the floor, said a crime-scene examination expert, and there was evidence of a blood trail leading from the bedroom to the garage. But White maintained his innocence from the time he was arrested.

In a videotaped interview with Homicide Detective Ernie Schreiber, White admits picking up the garbage bags in a grassy field and bringing them home, but he explains that he was just out looking at the areas to search the next day and thought he would clean up the litter. He also denied knowing what was inside the bags or seeing a lampshade matching the broken lamp on a post near the location he was seen picking up the bags.

White later took the stand, testifying in his own defence. The bloody materials found in the garbage bag came from a nosebleed, he said, caused when Liana was horsing around with their daughter. Liana was "dripping blood," so White said he used his T-shirt to wipe it off, then ran to get some paper towels to help clean up. He also grabbed a first-aid kit and used several pairs of latex gloves because Liana was worried about an infection and the gloves kept breaking. The testimony ended with White denying any responsibility for his wife's death or ever doing anything harmful to her.

"Never. I never ever laid a hand on her. I never hit her. I never beat her. I never pushed her. Nothing," he said, seeming close to tears. "I had everything. My world was right. I had the bull by the horns. Everything."

The following day, White continued to stick to his story under intense cross-examination. He admitted there were several inconsistencies in his interview with police, but he blamed them on being muddled over the shock of finding his pregnant wife's body and being charged with her death.

Despite his repeated claims of innocence, the seven women and five men on the jury found White guilty of second-degree murder after ten hours of deliberations. In December 2006, the twenty-nine-year-old was sentenced to life in prison with no chance of parole for seventeen years. White kept his head down, with his eyes sometimes closed, as Court of Queen's Bench Justice Mary Moreau handed down the sentence, calling the crime "brutal and callous."

"Mr. White committed the ultimate act of spousal abuse, while occupying a position of trust," said Justice Moreau. "Mr. White left the body without dignity in death, stripped naked in a ditch, exposed to the ravages of insects and scavenging animals."

Court documents released after the verdict added more disturbing details to an already heartbreaking story. The couple's daughter likely witnessed the attack and saw White cleaning up the bloody mess. She possibly even saw him disposing of the body and told her grandmother, "I've been here. My daddy took me here," when taken to the road where Liana's body was found.

On another occasion, the young girl told her grandmother that "Mommy said no more hitting [to] Daddy. And Daddy said 'yes,' hitting." When asked where her dad hit her mom, Ashley pounded on her tummy with her fist, then went to the wall and banged her head against it a couple of times, stating, "like that, Grandma." The girl also said there was blood on the floor "when Mommy died" and "Daddy cleaned it up with towels." Another chilling statement was

Liana White and her daughter, Ashley, in an undated family photo. (Photo courtesy of Sun Media)

made when Ashley said she'd "have to go and sleep in the leaves with my mommy" after seeing the husband of her grandmother's friend using a knife to cut buns. To avoid a threat of trial unfairness and the risk of misleading jurors, the jury did not hear any of Ashley's statements.

During the sentencing hearing, Maureen blasted White for ripping her family apart and coldheartedly denying his involvement in Liana's death. Maureen also spoke about Ashley, noting the girl wakes up in the middle of the night screaming for her mother and gets so emotional about it that she vomits.

"On July 12, 2005, my world fell apart when I received the call that is every mother's worst nightmare," she said, while reading her victim-impact statement before the court. Maureen's heart broke into a thousand pieces when Liana's body was found in the ditch. The heartache was overcome with extreme anger when White was charged with the hideous crime.

"I realized he had no remorse for what he had done. He had killed my daughter and was able to fool us all. He put my family through hell proclaiming his innocence," she said. "My blood boils, and my heart breaks over and over again. Dying this way is the worst thing that can happen to a person, and losing your own child this way is unimaginable."

Maintaining his innocence, White turned to Maureen and put her in charge of his daughter.

"Raise her well, like you raised Liana," he said. "Make sure she knows all about her, every little detail. And if it's not too much, tell her of the man I used to be, if you can ever find it in your heart."

White later appealed his conviction but lost his bid for a new trial.

Three years after Liana's death, the couple's suburban home still sat full of their belongings, even though nobody had lived there since White went to jail. It's not known why White killed Liana and ultimately destroyed his family, but it's a crime that will likely haunt his soul forever.

NO RHYME OR REASON

Cheryl Lynn Black lived a hard life. The forty-six-year-old small-framed woman, originally from the Siksika First Nation west of Calgary, was a convicted killer and alcoholic living on the streets of Edmonton, picking bottles to survive.

On May 18, 2004, Cheryl's hard life came to a violent end when somebody set her on fire and left her body in a dumpster behind the Walterdale Playhouse at 83rd Avenue and 103rd Street in Old Strathcona. A volunteer for the theatre found the remains in the dumpster, which was still hot, leading police to believe the fire was set sometime the day before.

Cheryl's body was so badly burned that it took three months for police to determine her identity. Since she had no teeth, hospital x-rays were used to find out her name. Evidence suggests Cheryl was still alive when she was set on fire.

Detective Ron Johnson of the Edmonton Police was one of the investigators working on the case. It was a crime scene he described with one word—"ugly."

"That was really grim," said Ron about the crime and the work involved to identify the victim. "There were no fingerprints to go on. We beat the bushes for a couple of months, checking on every small-framed [homeless] woman. We started with a list of ninety-eight and finally whittled them all down to Cheryl Black."

Who killed Cheryl remains a mystery, but she had made some enemies throughout the years. In 1992 she stabbed her thirty-one-year-old common-law husband, Greg Goodine, to death in the Calgary home they shared. She was convicted of second-degree murder, but was later sentenced to seven years for manslaughter. A family member later said Cheryl lived in fear that Greg's family would track her down for revenge. Finding her on the streets, however, wouldn't be an easy task.

Relatives on the reserve told a television news channel that Cheryl became an alcoholic after she claimed she was raped and beaten by a man her mother knew. The relatives also said she had a son in his twenties who lived the same lifestyle as his mother on the streets of Calgary.

As for finding the killer, Ron said police didn't have any witnesses to the crime, but there were a couple of leads

Cheryl Lynn Black's body was found in this burnt-out dumpster on May 18, 2004. (Photo by Tom Braid / Courtesy of Sun Media)

to follow. At one point he was convinced police did have a viable suspect. That man was picked up and interviewed, but he had a perfect, logical explanation for every question. Ron believes the murder was completely random.

"Those are always tough to solve," he said. "There is no rhyme or reason to it."

Former Edmonton Police Detective Ron Johnson holds a picture of Cheryl Lynn Black. (Photo by Tom Braid / Courtesy of Sun Media)

The murder of Carlos Mejia had no rhyme or reason either. In January 1999, Carlos's seventeen-year-old daughter found his body in his bedroom of the family's townhouse in northeast Edmonton. It was the city's first homicide of the year.

The last time his three teenaged daughters saw their dad was at around 10 p.m. on the night he died. They left him watching television alone in their home while they went to help a friend move. When they came home and saw his door closed, they assumed their father was sleeping.

Diana Melendez made the gruesome discovery the next day, when she went to wake her father up for work and found his blood-soaked body on his bedroom floor.

"I was in shock," she said. "I didn't know what to do."

Carlos died of stab wounds and multiple slashes to the neck. There was no sign of a struggle or any physical evidence left anywhere in the house. Police suspect someone paid the thirty-nine-year-old a visit sometime between 10 p.m. and 11:45 p.m. Neighbours said they heard loud thumping noises coming from the bedroom where Carlos's body was found but had chalked it up to noisy kids. The case stumped investigators, who had no significant leads.

"That was a brutal murder. There was no sign of forced entry," said Detective Ron Johnson, adding that the suspect could have been a surprised intruder.

"We never found anybody that [had anything against] the guy or he made an enemy out of. It was just a real 'who done it.'"

The single father had immigrated to Canada from El Salvador via Mexico in 1990. He was separated from his wife and living with his three daughters. Originally a painter, Carlos had gone back to school in recent years to become a welder. He enjoyed dancing and bodybuilding in his spare time, and he was last seen socially by his friends dancing at La Habana at 10238 104th Street on January 8, 1999.

Carlos's relatives said he had no enemies and they couldn't understand why anybody would want him dead.

"We never knew he had an enemy," said Maritza Mejia, Carlos's sister-in-law, a year after his death. "We will never forget what happened, but we could be proud the killer is in jail. That's our hope."

Carlos's death thrust Diana into adulthood the hard way. She took on a parental role to raise her two younger sisters, aged fourteen and sixteen, on her own, quitting school and getting a full-time job. Two years later, the girls had moved from the condo they once called home, but they didn't leave behind the memories of their father.

"I will never be happy again," said an emotional Diana, two years after her father's death. "We did everything together. He was a man with class, a man with style. He said if something like this were to ever happen that he'd never leave us. Maybe in my loneliness, in a sense, he's there too."

SHERNELL PIERRE AND NADINE ROBINSON-CREARY

Happy. Sad. Shocked. Those are the feelings Ishbel Cain experienced when she was told an arrest had been made in the murder of her twenty-six-year-old daughter, Shernell Sharon Pierre. Ishbel never lost hope that the day would come when police would arrest the person responsible for Shernell's horrific death four years earlier—but when that day arrived, it left her crippled with a wave of emotions.

On a Monday afternoon in March 2012, Ishbel was at her computer when she received a call from investigators, who told her that forty-three-year-old Devon Hugh Saunders— Shernell's ex-boyfriend—had been arrested and charged with first-degree murder. The news was shocking.

"My whole body went cold and I shivered," said Ishbel. "I believed this day would come, but how do you prepare for [it]? It was just a matter of time. Everything happens in God's own time, and this was his time."

It was just after 11 p.m. on March 12, 2008, when the friendly and upbeat Shernell left her job through the front doors of the Misericordia Hospital and walked to her vehicle—a Toyota Corolla she loved. About fifteen minutes later, the vehicle was found engulfed in flames on 170th

Street, just south of 87th Avenue, near the city's famous West Edmonton Mall. A woman working at the nearby mall was among the first to arrive at the scene.

"We didn't know at the time someone was inside. There were a lot of flames and it was pretty bad," she said. "My friend tried to get close to see if anyone was inside, but it was too hot and dangerous to get too close. I figured it was empty, but my friend kept saying that he thought someone was inside."

Investigators later revealed that Shernell had been fatally shot and her car doused with what appeared to be gasoline and set on fire, burning her body along with it. Fire officials said the flames reached higher than nine metres into the air—something that was very odd for a vehicle fire. The only thing that survived the fire was Shernell's Bible, which had pages torn out that were used as a wick to start the blaze. Shernell's sister, Jolin Thompson, doesn't believe the Bible's survival is a coincidence.

"It was a sign the Bible survived. It wasn't just by accident," said Jolin, who remembers Shernell as an easy-going, fun person who didn't cause any trouble. The pair spent much time together growing up in the Caribbean.

It didn't take long before police had a person of interest—someone who was seen at Shernell's car prior to the fire and who may have fled west from the scene of the crime. The person was described as a black male dressed in dark clothing. Detectives asked those living in the area to search their property for a gun that might have been tossed, along with clothing or a dark-coloured bag. By March 20, several persons of interest had been interviewed, but police wouldn't say if any of them were suspects.

Shernell and her family had moved to Canada from the island of St. Vincent when she was twelve years old.

In 2000 she graduated from Ross Sheppard Composite High School, where she had been active in track and field. She then went on to study nursing in college. The young woman had been working as a licensed practical nurse at the hospital for only about two years when she was murdered.

Those who knew Shernell described her as a woman who loved sports, church, and her family and friends. Her unit supervisor, Stephanie Ellis, said Shernell was always coming up with something to make people smile and laugh. Another colleague said they had never seen a day when Shernell wasn't smiling or joking around.

"Her fun-loving attitude is going to be greatly missed," said Stephanie. "She was a happy, fun-loving girl who was full of energy."

Investigators were on the cusp of making an arrest during the two years following Shernell's death. In February 2009, police had hoped the Crown prosecutor reviewing the case would give investigators the go-ahead to charge the person they believed was responsible for the crime, but that day didn't come until three years later.

Staff Sergeant Dennis Storey was the initial primary investigator on the case and said the accused came to the attention of police early in the investigation. Eventually, it was a combination of forensic evidence and interviews that finally led to an arrest—almost four years to the day that Shernell was murdered. Like Shernell's family, Dennis had been waiting for the moment he could announce that an arrest had been made.

"This was a very difficult investigation. The entire crime scene was consumed by fire. It takes time when you base a lot of your crime scene on forensic evidence and forensic experts." Although he was no longer in the homicide unit,

Dennis was the first to tell Saunders, previously unknown to police, that he was under arrest. "It's personally gratifying to any homicide investigator that can actually lay a charge," Dennis said. "It's nice to see this come to a conclusion."

In order to make an arrest, police reviewed countless hours of videotape, went through hundreds of telephone-call logs, and interviewed dozens of witnesses—some who only came forward a year after the murder. Dennis said the crime was so horrific, it generated a certain level of fear among witnesses. Eventually, however, those witnesses began to talk.

"We re-interviewed the witnesses and found new information. ... We were able to move this investigation further," said Dennis, who believed there were more people in the community with information that could have assisted in the investigation. Of the people who did come forward at the time, Dennis said, "I'd like to thank them for their help."

Like her mother, Jolin had mixed feelings about the arrest, but she had remained hopeful the day would eventually come. She was sad for her family and the family of the accused, whom she believed dated her sister for a couple of years. Jolin didn't know Saunders well, but the couple seemed happy, and everything seemed okay when they parted ways. With an arrest made, Jolin finally felt some closure, but the loss of her sister will never go away.

"I do miss her, but I've come to realize that she is gone; she's not coming back," she said. "I am sad that she's gone."

Ishbel, on the other hand, isn't sure if she'll ever have closure, knowing her daughter's life ended much too soon. "Even when everything is done and over with, would you ever have closure?" she said. "I don't know. I have never been through something like this before. Every day is different."

In April 2015, a Court of Queen's Bench justice found Saunders guilty of first-degree murder.

During a videotaped police interview played during the trial, Saunders denied having anything to do with the killing, but several of Shernell's co-workers testified that she told them Saunders was a jealous person and wasn't happy about the breakup. Shortly before her violent death, Shernell had begun a new relationship with a childhood friend.

In his opening statement, the Crown prosecutor told the court that Saunders got into Shernell's car after she got off work, then shot her while they were parked on 170th Street, just south of 87th Avenue. Saunders then doused Shernell and much of the car with gasoline and set it on fire before walking to West Edmonton Mall. An autopsy revealed that Shernell died from a gunshot wound to the head.

Glenmore Rennis, who had worked construction jobs with Saunders, testified that his colleague showed him on

Shernell Pierre. The twenty-six-year-old was fatally shot, then burned in her car, in March 2008. (Photo courtesy of Sun Media)

three occasions the .38-calibre revolver he carried around in his waistband. Glenmore also said Saunders told him several times that he sometimes felt like killing the nurse; he used to cry after she broke up with him, and she refused to take his calls. Another witness said he heard Saunders say, "I'm going to kill that girl," following an unhappy phone conversation he overheard between Saunders and Shernell.

While Saunders was under surveillance, police recovered a glove he tossed into a dumpster. The gunshot residue on the glove further tied Saunders to the case. In the end, he was sentenced to life in prison with no chance of parole for twenty-five years.

"Justice has been served," said Jolin, outside of court after the verdict. "I never once gave up hope."

As one family tries to recover from a nightmare, another continues to wait for that phone call from police.

Nadine Robinson-Creary worked as a licensed practical nurse at the Royal Alexandra Hospital when she was found dead by her brother and stepson in her Clareview townhouse near 139th Avenue and 32nd Street on July 20, 2006. To date, no persons of interest have been identified, and the cause of the thirty-six-year-old's death has never been released—not even to her own family.

"All we know is that she died. We don't know how or why—and it's so hard," said her sister, Kendra Robinson, around the fifth anniversary of the murder. "I know I feel very defeated. It feels so hopeless."

Prior to her death, tiny, Jamaica-born Nadine had rekindled a relationship with her husband, Wayne Creary, following a thirteen-year separation. During an interview with a newspaper in July 2006, Wayne said he had nothing to do with his wife's death, adding that he was putting his faith in God and the police to bring those responsible to justice.

"You can hide things from man, but you can't hide things from God...and God is my judge. People can say what they want...if you know your hands are clean and your heart is clean, you're serving someone greater than man," said Wayne, a tall, slender, bespectacled man, who spoke softly and slowly. He did not cry, but excused himself from the interview once, when asked about his life in Jamaica during the separation, to which he would not comment. But he did say, "It's like losing [a part of your body]. It's going to be a long, long grieving process."

Wayne was reportedly absent from his wife's funeral, but insisted that he attended the service in secrecy because

Kevin Robinson sits by a picture of his sister, Nadine Robinson-Creary, who was found dead in her Edmonton townhouse on July 20, 2006. (Photo courtesy of Sun Media)

of his overwhelming grief and a desire to avoid confrontation with other family members, many of whom attended from the U.S. and Jamaica. His wife's ability to "pull things together no matter what" and her "heart as big as the universe" is what he said he missed the most, adding, "She didn't deserve to die like that."

In the mean time, the Robinsons continue to celebrate their loved one's life by holding an annual barbecue in her memory. Her mother, Antonette Robinson, will never lose hope that one day her daughter's killer will spend the rest of their life behind bars.

"It's very hard on the whole family," said Antonette, who last saw her daughter heading to work on July 19, 2006, in her red Chevrolet Cavalier.

"We just need someone to say something. That's what we're waiting for. Police are just at a standstill right now, waiting for somebody to come forth. They don't want to do anything until they have [something] concrete."

THE MANDINS

Susan Mandin and her husband, Maurice, were passionate about life. The couple not only shared a love for their family, but also adored the great outdoors, which prompted them to purchase a farmhouse near Valleyview, Alberta, as a get-away property for weekend adventures and summer vacations.

The pair had big dreams for the small three-bedroom farmhouse located on several acres of land approximately three hundred kilometres northwest of the city. It's where they wanted to spend their retirement and hoped their children would join them some day by building cottages of their own.

One day in the summer of 1991, the family—Susan, Maurice, and their two daughters—left the farm for a few hours to go on a shopping trip. Susan's fifteen-year-old son, Gavin, had elected to stay behind. While the family was away, the teen fumed over what he perceived as unjust treatment resulting from a series of relatively minor incidents. He became so enraged that he decided to kill his mother and stepfather when they returned, and he was waiting for them as they pulled into the farmyard.

As Maurice got out of the family car, Gavin shot him in the head with a small-calibre rifle from a window inside the home. Frightened by the shots, Gavin's mother and two sisters, Janelle, ten, and Islay, twelve, remained in the vehicle, ducking down to take cover. Gavin waited for his mother to poke her head back up, then shot her while his two terrified sisters remained in the back seat of the car.

The teen then approached his injured stepfather, shooting him a second time, delivering a fatal blow. He then shot his two sisters at close range, killing both of them. The angry youth continued shooting his victims multiple times, pulling the trigger until the gun was empty.

Once the bullets stopped flying, Gavin got a knife and cut open his mother's flowered blue dress, panties, and bra to expose her naked body. He bound his stepfather's body with rope, and dragged it behind an ATV for nearly a mile to a meadow, then returned home. The vehicle containing his murdered mother and two sisters was driven to a nearby treeline and abandoned, in an effort to hide his gruesome crime.

The teen remained in the house for another day and a half before leaving in the family van with a cooler, two knives, a shotgun, and the rifle he'd used in the shootings. Several hours later, he was stopped by police concerned about his driving. Gavin, however, stomped on the gas when officers wanted to examine the vehicle, sparking a high-speed chase that reached speeds of 170 kilometres per hour. Eventually he was stopped and taken into custody, later confessing to the murders.

The deaths of four people at the hands of a teenager was as hard to comprehend for the quiet community of Valleyview as it was for residents of St. Albert—a small city on the outskirts of Edmonton, where the family's primary residence was located. Described by neighbours as a devoted Christian, forty-one-year-old Susan was a deacon in her St. Albert church, where she helped her congregation wherever possible. Her children meant the world to her. Maurice was into cycling and running and, like Susan, was a teacher with Edmonton Public Schools. The principal of Delwood Elementary School, where Maurice taught French immersion for three years, considered having a school counselor talk to students. News of the slayings was a terrible shock.

"He always had a little smile, always had a little joke," the principal said. "He had a good sense of humour." The couple's neighbours were lost for words.

"My God, I don't believe it," said a neighbour with tears in her eyes. "Those two little girls. They used to come over and play with the dogs. He [Maurice] was a very nice fellow. Every so often, I'd see him going off on his bike, and I'd say hi. She [Susan] was very well-educated and a woman who was a good mother. She cared about her children."

Teachers and friends of Gavin—a teen with large round glasses and acne-prone skin—couldn't believe the "quiet and funny" boy had been accused of murdering his entire family. A friend was certain that police had the wrong person in custody. Staff at his school never had any concerns about the student with an IQ of 133.

"I think it was someone else—someone violent who was trying to rob them," said the schoolmate. "He was quiet but funny. He liked comedy movies. One of the funniest things is his laugh. He is just hilarious."

Gavin was found fit to stand trial and eventually convicted of four counts of second-degree murder, despite his pleas of not guilty. He was sentenced as an adult, receiving a life sentence with no eligibility of parole for ten years.

Gavin later stated that he was motivated to commit the murders by the resentment and anger he felt toward his mother, whom he viewed as too controlling. At the age of five, Gavin's parents separated, and he lived with his mother. Five years later, she married Maurice.

During hearings with the Parole Board of Canada, Gavin explained that he developed a hatred toward his mother from a very young age, but he wasn't completely sure why he felt such strong hostility. He resented her efforts to control him, felt she was very demanding and placed high expectations on him, yet he craved his mother's love and acceptance, resenting the attention she gave his sisters. At the same time, Gavin rejected his mother's attempts to reach out to him with any kind of loving gesture. As Gavin became a teenager, his anger and frustration grew, causing him to withdraw from the family and bury himself in books and video games. Over the years, he blamed his mother for all of the negative experiences in his life.

The board first met with Gavin in 2001 for full parole consideration, but determined that his risk was not manageable, so a conditional release was denied. Relatives of the murdered family attended the hearings at the Bowden Institution, hoping to see some sign of compassion in the killer's eyes. Instead, they walked away filled with disappointment.

"We all wanted to see some progress...that he could be a safe, contributing member of society. But he had his back to us the whole time. He didn't look at us at all," said his aunt, Collette Mandin-Kossowan, who hadn't seen him since the trial.

"He never mentioned my brother. He never mentioned his sisters. He talked about his mother. He said he lived with a hatred of his mother that was all-consuming and all-encompassing. These are his words."

When asked by the board if he was sorry for the slayings, an emotionless Gavin stated, "Remorse is something that's always been a challenge to me. I do still see myself as a victim of my parents." Through tears after the hearing, Gavin's grandfather said all indications are "this young man's a psychopath."

Earlier psychological and psychiatric assessments suggested Gavin was indeed psychopathic. This, however, was disputed in a later report that suggested the shooting was an isolated incident, but the report added that Gavin still displayed narcissistic tendencies consistent with abnormal personality traits.

In 2009 the board met with Gavin again. This time he was authorized a series of unescorted temporary absences to a halfway house for personal development, to be taken over a one-year period. Three years later, when he was thirty-six years old, Gavin was granted day parole. The news was unsettling for his surviving family members who had suffered lifelong effects due to his violent actions that day in August 1991.

In victim-impact statements, family members said they hadn't had peace or tranquility since the murders. They spoke of experiencing horror, anger, uncontrollable weeping, devastation, post-traumatic stress, chronic grief, a lost sense of security, irreparable damage, distrust, unshakable pervasive fear, nightmares, and depression. One family member said she was afraid to have children of her own, claiming she felt she wouldn't be able to trust them. Every new parole process reignited the horror of her family's murder.

"We [had] a very close-knit family," said Monique Mandin following the murders. The eldest of Maurice's children from a previous marriage, Monique said there was no division between her and her two brothers and Susan's younger daughters from a previous marriage.

"They were my sisters," Monique said. "Islay was loving and nurturing—a mature young child. I always forgot she was only twelve years old. She could relate to anyone, from babies to their 106-year-old Nana.....I'd always wanted little sisters and I got two."

The decision to grant a mass murderer day parole wasn't arrived at without a few reservations. The board struggled with the fact that Gavin persisted in maintaining a victim stance, and he continued heaping blame upon his mother for his problems. He showed little regret for his actions and also had yet to fully comprehend the gravity of the offences, but through programming and counseling, the board believed, Gavin had developed a degree of emotional maturity and some insight into the aberrant and narcissistic thinking that characterized him as a teenager. By this time, Gavin had spent twenty years behind bars, participating in numerous programs to prepare him for life on the outside.

"During your hearing you impressed as being candid and open about why you offended as you did and how you have come to terms with your actions," wrote the board in its decision. "You have not been able to rationally explain why you killed your sisters, but it appears that you will never fully explain this action."

Today, Gavin continues to receive day parole and goes by the name Gavin Ian Maclean, taking the names of his biological father. He continues to be banned from having any contact with the families of the deceased, with the exception of one person who's supported him from the beginning. He must also report any attempts to initiate relationships with females to his parole supervisor.

The most recent parole report in 2013 stated that Gavin had been demonstrating perfectionism and commitment to release, being polite and respectful with staff and residents of his halfway house. Call-ins and spot checks had been accurately verified, and he'd been diligent in completing his daily itinerary and updating staff of his whereabouts at all times. Gavin had also been participating socially with two community groups of people who share common interests and hobbies. Finding employment, however, in his field of computer technology had been a challenge.

"Overall your parole officer indicates you have demonstrated good progress towards developing yourself in the community, especially noting you were incarcerated for a long time beginning as a youth," wrote the board in the report. "You have made a good start at reintegrating into the community. Clearly, this will not be an easy or short term process and it is critical that you set attainable goals as you continue to reside in the community so that you will not be emotionally overwhelmed at any stage."

Numerous psychological and psychiatric reports have identified Gavin as a low risk for violent offending and a low to moderate risk for general offending. Nonetheless, he must follow psychological counseling arranged by his parole supervisor to address the areas of personal/emotional orientation and issues with re-entering a society he hasn't known for more than two decades.

It's not known where Gavin is living, but family members believe he's still in Ontario, where he was moved to another prison several years ago. Only time will tell whether or not Gavin can truly become a productive, regular member of society after, as an angry teen, he murdered his own family.

Every night that Izaac Middleton went out with his friends, his mother, Ruth—like a typical parent of a teenager—would worry about his safety. But on the night of September 19, 1997, those worries turned into every parent's worst nightmare. Ruth was in a deep sleep when she heard sirens roaring in the distance. Then the police showed up at her front door and delivered the grim news that her eighteen-year-old son was never coming home.

"They said, 'He's been in an accident.' They told me that he had died," said Ruth. "I just started screaming and then [Izaac's] girlfriend [who was living downstairs at the time] came upstairs and my [other] son, and we just didn't believe it."

Izaac was stabbed in the heart by a mob of men on the train tracks south of what was known as the Thunderdome Bar at 99th Street and Argyll Road. According to a friend who was with him that night, more than ten drunk and rowdy men who were leaving the bar picked a fight with Izaac and his friends in the parking lot. Izaac grabbed a bat from the trunk of his car for protection, but he was outnumbered. The mob followed Izaac and two friends to the tracks where the fatal attack occurred.

Detectives believed Izaac's murder should have been an open-and-shut case, but it has sat on the books unsolved for nearly twenty years because witnesses won't talk, despite a $40,000 reward for information leading to the killer.

"The one who did the stabbing is going to have to live with it for the rest of his life, and the people who witnessed it and truly know what happened have to live with it, too," said Homicide Detective Doug Fisher a couple of years after Izaac's death. A man from the attacking group who was also stabbed during the melee, although not fatally, wouldn't cooperate with police, either, the detective added. "It's that old proverbial attitude—hear no evil and see no evil when it comes to my friends."

Izaac Middleton. (Photo courtesy of Sun Media)

"I've narrowed it down to three to five people. I thought going into this... we'd be successful in solving it. It's frustrating."

Not long after he got his first job working at a bingo hall, Izaac found out his girlfriend, Erin Bradley, was pregnant. The couple planned to live in his mother's basement and continue going to school while raising the child, but Izaac never got the chance to meet his daughter, Justice, who was named after the one thing in the world Erin wants most.

"I used to look at her sometimes and cry," she said, a couple of years after Izaac's death. "We need them to be brought to justice. Then we'd have someone to blame, but it seems like a dead issue," she added, speaking of the frustration she shared with Doug Fisher.

Following the death of her oldest son, Ruth spiraled into a deep depression. She gets emotional when talking about Izaac and thinks about him every day. "Our whole family has changed," she said. "We know he's missing. Even at Christmas we try and put on a front, but we know he's not there. That's why we try and keep his memory going with the birthdays and anniversary."

Each year, Izaac's birthday is celebrated with about thirty of his friends and family. They gather in a park for a barbecue and share stories about the young man, who enjoyed playing hockey and football. Izaac was a goaltender and was sponsored for two years to play for a hockey team. He also played bantam and midget football and was once voted an MVP. The two friends who were with Izaac the night he died always attend the barbecue. One of them credits Izaac for saving his life. He named his son after Izaac.

Ruth admits Izaac got into trouble with police over "dumb stuff" in his early teens, but he was changing his life in anticipation of becoming a father. Izaac was never one to start fights, she said, but he wasn't one to back down from them either.

"He always stood up if someone was on him or his brother. It took him a long time to get mad, but to defend somebody, he would be [in] there like a [dirty] shirt," she said.

Ruth never imagined that nearly twenty years would pass and the case would remain unsolved. Two of Izaac's attackers have since passed away, she said, but the one she believes delivered the fatal wound is still out there living his life. Someday, Ruth hopes the killer will confess to what he's done so she can let him know how much her family has suffered as a result of his actions that fateful September night.

"We know he's still out there," she said, adding that she still hopes for some resolution to the case after all these years. "It would be great to relieve some of this." And Ruth isn't necessarily after revenge. "I don't want anything to happen to him [the one responsible]," she said, pleading, "Just admit what you did. I just want justice done. I want closure."

Doug has since retired, and the case is now in the hands of Detective Howie Antoniuk with the Edmonton Police historical homicide unit. The file is still open, but there haven't been any tips for a number of years. A code of silence could keep it that way indefinitely.

"It's frustrating for all of us," said Howie. "People don't talk to us and the family wants results, and you can't blame the family for wanting results. Hopefully somebody will have a change of heart and talk to us at some point in time about it and give us that one piece of information we need to move forward and conclude [the case] successfully."

Izaac's case is eerily similar to another unsolved murder that took place in the city four months earlier. In May 1997, James Milliken was enjoying a night out with three friends at the Beverly Crest Hotel in north Edmonton. His best friend, Stacy Byrne, was among the crew.

Stacy and James met in their north Edmonton neighbourhood when they were sixteen years old, forming a special bond that lasted into adulthood. On that particular night in May, the four friends were out on the weekend, blowing off steam. The fun, however, came to an end when they were asked to leave the bar after one of them got in trouble with a bouncer.

On the way home, outside a nearby convenience store, the four friends were confronted by a mob of sixteen youths who were members of the notorious Northside gang. One of them came up to the group and demanded a cigarette.

"It wasn't, 'Can I borrow one,' it was, 'Give me a smoke,'" said Stacy. "We told him to go screw himself."

The comment sparked a brawl that spilled into the Abbottsfield Mall parking lot near 118th Avenue and 34th Street. One of the gang members pulled out a butterfly knife and started swinging it around, nicking Stacy across the top of the head. James came over to Stacy's aid, but then twenty-three-year-old James was fatally wounded.

"I was going down and then they gave me a booting for a bit," Stacy recalled. "I was knocked out when the paramedics were just arriving. I blanked out for a bit until they came and told me he was gone. It was the worst feeling in the world."

The day after James's murder, Jason Riley Laronde turned himself in to police. He was charged with second-degree murder and possession of a weapon, but those charges were eventually stayed by the Crown due to problems with witnesses positively identifying the killer. The situation was further muddied when another Northside gang member took the stand during Laronde's preliminary hearing and claimed he was the one who killed James.

As the weeks turned into months, Stacy lost hope the killer would ever be brought to justice. He believes police sold James out in an effort to get rid of the Northside gang.

"I think they made a deal with this gang just shortly afterwards, because the gang disbanded and wasn't really heard from," Stacy said. "Leading up to it, they were in the news a lot. They made a deal—nobody gets charged with anything, and you guys just go away and stop causing trouble."

Police agreed the gang was quiet following James's death, but said it was likely because detectives were paying more attention to the "bunch of punks," who considered the murder to be "like a badge" of honour.

A year after James's murder, friends and family broke down in a flood of tears as they gathered at the site of his death to say a final collective goodbye. They retraced what were probably James's last steps across the parking lot, then they laid a stack of white carnations and pale-yellow roses in his memory.

"He wasn't just some guy," said his common-law wife, Cathy, who was six months pregnant with the couple's child when James died. "He had a family, he had a son, he was a person—he was somebody."

James Milliken. He was fatally stabbed when he and three friends became involved in an altercation with twelve to fifteen males in north Edmonton. (Photo courtesy of Sun Media)

"I don't understand how somebody could get away with this," added James's sister during the same gathering. "It's hard knowing the person who did this to you is walking around free as a bird, laughing at the system."

With a $50,000 reward up for grabs, the family remained hopeful that somebody might come forward with information about the crime to move the investigation ahead.

The case remained unsolved for nearly eighteen years until, finally, new information resulted in the Medicine Hat Police Service taking a man into custody. A charge of second-degree murder and possession of a prohibited weapon were laid against thirty-seven-year-old Darren Jason Young. At this writing, the case is before the courts.

Police said Young was a suspect from the first few days of the investigation, but there wasn't sufficient evidence to lay charges against him at the time. In a statement, James's family said the arrest came as a great relief: "[The arrest] will hopefully provide us answers to questions we have; questions that have haunted us for years. The arrest will not help us deal with our grief—there is no justice. Jimmy is dead, but perhaps some closure can now begin."

When Stacy thinks about his best friend, he can't help but think about all the good times they had together. James was a great guy, he said, and it was always fun whenever he was around. James's son, James Skylar, born three months after his father was murdered, reminds Cathy of James's death every day. "He's just like his dad," Stacy said. Stacy stayed with Cathy for support in the months following James's murder and continues to keep in touch with the family.

CONSTABLE EZIO FARAONE

On a hot afternoon in June 1990, a trio of robbery detectives closely watched a suspicious car roll up to the intersection of 124th Street and 107th Avenue. Squinting through the bright sunlight, the officers recognized that the vehicle was the same colour as the one used in two holdups the previous week at a Royal Bank on the corner. The odds of the bank being hit a third time didn't seem favourable.

The detectives were focused on the Royal Bank when one of them suddenly saw a masked man armed with a shotgun run from the Bank of Nova Scotia across the street.

Minutes earlier, Sonya Booth was in the bank helping a customer with a certified cheque when a man with nylon over his head burst through the door and told everybody to get down on the floor. Crouching on the ground near her teller's wicket, Sonya looked up to see the robber vault the counter and land next to her. He demanded she open the cash drawers.

"I stood up and he brought the gun in my face," she said, noting the weapon had a big hole in the end. "I was frozen and couldn't move and he said, 'Let's move it, baby.'"

Sonya and another teller emptied their money drawers and tossed marked bills known as bait money into the robber's red-and-navy sports bag. A surveillance camera was also secretly activated, snapping two shots of the masked man.

When the robber realized he couldn't get into the bank vault, he became frustrated, jumped the counter, and fled the scene. The detectives outside watched the masked man dive into the back seat of a red Dodge Colt. The driver gunned the engine and roared away with the police in pursuit.

The tactical unit was called on a private channel used for special operations to assist in a high-risk vehicle stop to be conducted with a minimum of four officers. Constable Ezio Faraone was one of the tactical officers called to help with the pursuit of the getaway car. The thirty-three-year-old was driving behind task-force team leader Detective Ernie Schreiber when he noticed the Colt take a detour. Ezio followed the vehicle into an alley near 124th Street and 117th Avenue, but the lane was blocked at the south end by construction, forcing the car to come to a stop.

Despite a police policy that requires officers to notify others by radio before leaving their cars—especially when they're alone in high-risk situations—Ezio got out of his cruiser without doing so to try to make the arrest.

With his weapon drawn, the officer approached the car and confronted the driver, who stepped outside with his hands raised. Ezio was unaware that the man armed with the sawed-off shotgun was hiding in the back seat.

From a distance of about one metre, the gunman fired two blasts at Ezio, hitting him once in the upper abdomen and then again in the head. The first shot left a three-centimetre hole in the officer's chest, surrounded by a large number of small round holes. Ezio was killed almost instantly.

Gravel truck operator Dale Wells saw the officer approach the driver, then heard two shots in quick succession.

When the coast seemed clear, he jumped out of his truck and found the officer lying crumpled on the concrete, still clutching his service revolver that hadn't been fired. Blood was flowing from his severe wounds.

"The police officer never had a chance," said Dale.

Workers replacing sewers in the area saw one suspect take off in the car while the other ran down the alley. The vehicle squeezed by three gravel trucks waiting in the lane, then cut across a grassy area, bouncing over a piece of wood. A backhoe operator tried to stop the car, but the small hatchback slipped past and roared away.

Construction workers began chasing the suspect who was fleeing on foot. The long-haired fugitive ran south along the alley, then doubled back to an apartment building on the northeast corner of 117th Avenue and 124th Street.

Robbery Detective Stuart Tutt was on his way to the Bank of Nova Scotia, when an ambulance whizzed by at a high rate of speed. He decided to follow the emergency vehicle into a lane behind 11622 123rd Street, where he was stopped by an individual who said he saw a man with a gun run into a nearby apartment building. Another individual said someone had been shot in the alley. Stuart had arrived in the alley to find several construction workers running around, pointing in different directions. Many of them had witnessed the shooting. Stuart also discovered Ezio's police cruiser and the officer's lifeless body.

"It was evident he was dead. I recognized him, but I didn't know his name," said Stuart. "I got a police blanket and covered him up."

Sergeant Vern Colley arrived at the scene shortly after Stuart. Members of Ezio's task-force team were still calling him on the radio.

"I went over and pulled the blanket back, and I recognized the man as an officer who had worked for me—Ezio Faraone," said Vern. "I had the task of telling those members, please stop calling because Constable Faraone is not coming."

Ernie was unaware that his colleague had been shot dead when a passerby pointed out one of the suspects casually walking along 122nd Street minutes after the blasts were fired. The detective pulled out his gun and soon had the man in handcuffs. While frisking him for weapons, $3,789 was found tucked inside his jeans. Seventeen bills matched the serial numbers of the money swiped from the bank. Another officer found $2,031 strewn around the backyard of a nearby home where the getaway car had been stashed. The second suspect was arrested a few hours later at an apartment near 135th Avenue and 38th Street. Both suspects were dotted with fresh needle marks and appeared to be high on drugs.

Ezio was a ten-year veteran of the Edmonton Police Service and had earned his position on Squad C of the prestigious, twenty-eight-member specialized tactical team unit whose job was to respond to high-risk crisis situations. The unit's members had to come to terms with the possibility of facing life-and-death situations, but no member had lost their life until that afternoon of June 25, 1990.

Ezio's death marked the first time in more than seven decades that an Edmonton police officer had been slain in the line of duty. The last officers killed on the job were Constable William Dixon in 1919 and Constable Frank Beevers in 1918. Dixon was shot by a man loitering near a building downtown, and Beevers was shot while struggling with a suspected murderer.

Ezio's cold-blooded killing was devastating for many members of the police service. He had been known as the funniest guy on the task force, who loved to joke around and weave stories. His laugh was contagious and got everyone going.

"He was a happy guy, a terrific person. He got along with everybody," said Sergeant Bruce Cruickshank, a member of the task force at the time. "It's a tragic loss. Everybody's feeling it. It's like the loss of a family member, not a work associate."

In addition to supporting his co-workers with his sense of humour, Ezio also always remembered his friends' birthdays and special occasions. There was nothing about his character that needed to be sugar-coated.

"He would call your home when you were sick and check on your welfare. He would call regularly to see how you and the children were doing. He would call even wives of friends to wish them happy birthday," said Staff Sergeant Hugh Richards, Ezio's supervisor and close friend.

More than a thousand people, including police officers from across the country, attended Ezio's funeral service in Edmonton. Hundreds more waited outside the church, which was only about fifteen blocks from where he was killed. A smaller burial mass also took place in a Roman Catholic Church in the Vancouver suburb of Burnaby, B.C., where Ezio was raised.

Jerry Crews, twenty-three, and Albert Foulston, twenty-seven, were both charged with first-degree murder. Adding salt to the wound was that one of the accused was out on mandatory supervision, and the other was out on full parole.

Two months prior to the shooting, Crews had been released from Edmonton Institution on mandatory supervision after serving two-thirds of a sentence. Foulston was released on day parole about a year earlier; his release status had been upgraded to full parole the previous December.

Many people in the community began questioning why Foulston was out on city streets in the first place. The career criminal's record dates back to the early 1980s and lists forty-nine convictions, including two for robberies in Edmonton in 1983. He also has a history of being unable to complete a single sentence without committing another crime. Two months before the murder, Foulston violated his parole by driving impaired, but the parole board decided to continue his full parole instead of returning him to jail, even though he had twice violated earlier releases on day parole. The record of his partner-in-crime—who he met in prison—wasn't much better.

Ever since Crews left his Nova Scotia home at the age of fifteen, he had been addicted to alcohol and drugs, living the life of a drifter, and committing crimes like house break-ins and theft. In 1987 he was given four years behind bars for illegally entering a dwelling, possession of a firearm, assault with a weapon, and obstructing justice in Calgary. On two occasions, he was denied day parole and full parole prior to his release on mandatory supervision in April 1990. During the time he did spend behind bars, Crews regularly abused illicit drugs and continued his habit upon his release, selling drugs for income.

The province's solicitor general was asked for an immediate public inquiry into the circumstances surrounding the officer's death. The National Parole Board launched an internal investigation as well. Edmonton Police did the same, addressing the question of single-officer patrol cars, but Police Chief Doug McNally wasn't sure if a second officer would have made any difference.

"I suppose we could 'if' ourselves to death with a question like that," he said. "Perhaps if two constables had been in the car we would have two dead constables instead of one. Perhaps it would have made a difference."

In the months following Ezio's untimely death, more police officers began donning bulletproof vests as part of their regular uniform. Prior to the shooting, about 60 per cent of police wore the vests regularly; afterward, about 85 per cent were wearing the protective gear. In downtown Edmonton, a 1.7-hectare park was named in Ezio's honour. It featured a life-sized bronze sculpture of the officer holding the hand of a child. It was made possible largely through donations from the community.

More than a year after the shooting, Foulston and Crews were ordered to stand trial in Court of Queen's Bench. Foulston, however, challenged an earlier court decision to stand trial for first-degree murder, since he didn't pull the trigger. A judge later ruled he would be tried for manslaughter instead.

During the fourteen-day trial, witness Heather Orvell shared more details about the moment Ezio was gunned down. She told the court she was watching television in her apartment suite on 124th Street near 116th Avenue when she heard sirens outside. She went to a window overlooking the alley and spotted a police cruiser and a maroon car ahead of it. A dump truck was blocking their passage down the lane.

The police officer got out of his cruiser and pointed a gun at the maroon car while yelling at the driver to get out with his hands on his head. Heather watched the driver obey the officer's commands as he stumbled around the car, then he stopped on a driveway in front of a garage near the officer. At that point, Heather saw somebody in the back seat of the car. The door opened ever so slowly and revealed a man holding a gun.

"The officer looked like he was just about to go up to the driver. He came out from behind his [car] door and was just about to arrest him. I guess, all of a sudden I heard shots," said Heather.

"The officer went down, his legs came out from underneath him and he went down," she added. "The driver of the car didn't check Faraone or even look back at him."

In addition to the statements of several witnesses who saw the shooting, police also collected plenty of evidence from the Dodge Colt and the murder weapon. Crews's fingerprints were found on the sawed-off shotgun, which was discovered under a barbecue at the rear of a house at 113th Avenue and 122nd Street. Inside the Colt parked behind the house, police seized a wallet containing a driver's licence and Alberta Health Care card in Crews's name. A thumbprint identified as Crews's was found on one of the car's windows. Another print, identified as Foulston's, was lifted from a matchbook inside the vehicle. Investigators also found nylon stockings and a duffle bag containing a shotgun shell and $187 cash.

During testimony, an undercover officer said he recognized Foulston as the driver of the red Colt he saw circling the area of the Bank of Nova Scotia. Moments later, the officer saw someone with his head covered by a stocking running out of the bank.

Testifying in his own defence, Crews told the court he hadn't slept for six days and seven nights leading up to the shooting. Wired on cocaine that morning, Crews injected a tranquilizer to help him sleep. He later woke up just before noon. Before Crews headed to a meeting with his probation officer at 3 p.m., he and Foulston drove to 124th Street and 107th Avenue to check out a bank they wanted to rob in the future.

"But I got there and saw it and said it looks too easy, so I did it," said Crews. The pair didn't realize police were even on their tail until Crews looked back and saw a set of flashing red lights.

When Foulston's car got trapped by the construction equipment in the alley, Crews claimed he was prepared to surrender and started getting out of the vehicle until the constable yelled, "No, just the driver." He said he planned to throw the shotgun on the ground and had no intentions of shooting the officer or even aiming the gun at him. All he said he remembered was the shotgun lying in his lap as he sat in the back seat of the getaway car while his friend walked toward the constable in the alley.

"Then there was a bang. I thought it came from the dump truck or something and I turned to see what it was and I looked back again," said Crews.

"All I saw was the policeman down in the crouch. The next thing I saw was a heat-wave flash come out of the end of the gun. I didn't hear the gun go off. I looked down and saw the gun shell being ejected out of it."

After three days of deliberations, the seven-woman, five-man jury convicted Crews of first-degree murder and Foulston of manslaughter. Both men were also found guilty of armed robbery and unlawful use of a firearm. The pair sat stone-faced in the prisoners' box, Crews letting out a sigh and bowing his shoulders slightly once the verdict was read. He was later sentenced to life in prison with no chance of parole for twenty-five years. Moments before Foulston was sentenced to twenty years in jail, he stood and defiantly proclaimed his innocence.

"I feel my case has been highly publicized. I've been incriminated and I've been sentenced and everything else due to the press and that's all I've got to say," he said before hesitating for a second. "And beside, I'm not guilty of the charges."

Court of Queen's Bench Justice Alexander Andrekson noted Foulston never expressed remorse for what happened and showed callous disregard for Ezio Faraone as he died at his feet.

"As soon as the police officer was hit by the shotgun fired by Mr. Crews, you were seen escaping the scene without the slightest concern or regard for the welfare of the police officer, who lay near where you were standing," said Justice Andrekson, noting Foulston's fifty-one offences on his criminal record before the shooting. "Your behaviour is unacceptable and must be repudiated by society."

A couple of weeks before her brother was gunned down, Jo-Anne Quarto phoned to tell him she was four months pregnant with her fifth child. Ezio never got to meet his nephew—Ezio Patrick Quarto—whose name now helps keep the fallen officer's memory alive. Quarto's oldest son often talks about his uncle Ezio, who took him golfing when he visited in 1989. Ezio was just starting to consider having a family of his own when his life was suddenly cut short.

"He just brightened our lives when he was here,"

Constable Ezio Faraone, fatally shot in June 1990 following a robbery at an Edmonton Bank of Nova Scotia branch. (Photo courtesy of Sun Media)

his sister said following the jury's conviction. "He would always see the funny side of a situation. No matter what kind of mood you were in, he was always uplifting."

"It's hardest on Mom," she added. "We're glad that this part of it is over, but we're still very sad. We have to go on with the sorrow in our hearts and we're doing the best that we can. We'll never forget him, though."

Fifteen years after the shooting, Ezio's death remains fresh in the mind of Tony Simioni. The Edmonton Police sergeant was at the scene that day, and it chilled him to the core. He can never go back to the area where Ezio was killed without thinking about what happened. When he thinks about Crews, and particularly Foulston, Tony's blood boils.

In September 2009, Foulston was released to an Edmonton halfway house after serving two-thirds of his twenty-year manslaughter sentence. The release of the then forty-eight-year-old caused an uproar, prompting then Edmonton Police Chief Mike Boyd to write a letter to the chairman of the National Parole Board in Ottawa, asking for an intervention in the case to suspend or terminate Foulston's statutory release. The career criminal, however, was let back out on city streets once again.

Just days into 2011, Foulston was back behind bars for violating the conditions of his statutory release. Tony's only surprise was that it didn't happen sooner. He believes Foulston is a man who should never be let out of jail.

"This person has had a lifetime of failed releases and is a danger to the public," Tony said. "They continue to exercise these releases and try to sell it on the mistaken fact that they have no choice, but that is absurd. Lock him up and don't let him out. Make him serve every single day of his sentence, which is what the public expects."

n July 2004, Ron Campbell was reading the newspaper at his kitchen table when he came across an article about a fiery collision involving a Sherwood Park truck driver near Golden, B.C. The man's legs became pinned inside the vehicle, which burst into flames. Another driver came to the rescue, but it was no use: the trucker burned to death.

When Ron's wife walked into the kitchen and said something to him, he didn't respond. She turned around to scold her husband for ignoring her, then noticed the tears streaming down his face.

"She asked what was wrong and I told her this story [the one in the newspaper]," said Ron, a staff sergeant with the RCMP in Edmonton. Twenty-two years earlier, Ron had been involved in the same kind of situation as a young constable. That memory was still very much alive.

"I can still hear him screaming. I can remember the smells. I can remember to this day visually the people that were there. I ran to the truck, and this man grabbed me by the right arm and said, 'Don't even think about it, young fella, we don't need to.' And we stood and watched."

Five months before he broke down that day in the kitchen, Ron had watched a mentally ill gunman kill RCMP dog handler Corporal Jim Galloway.

Around 2 p.m. on February 28, 2004, officers arrived at a Spruce Grove home thirty kilometres west of Edmonton to investigate a report of a bullet hole in a vehicle. While police were looking at the vehicle, a woman ran out of a nearby home and frantically advised the officers to get out of the area. A man inside the house was agitated and had a gun.

The RCMP emergency response team was immediately called to seal off the area, and nearby residents were told to either leave their homes or stay in their basements.

The gunman, Martin Ostopovich, called a television station and said he had had enough of the crap he had been taking from police and someone was going to die. Negotiators were in touch with Ostopovich inside his home for several hours, but shortly after 6 p.m., he burst outside and made for his truck, carrying two long-barreled rifles.

Ostopovich backed out of the driveway, but Jim and his partner, Constable Tim Taniguchi, rammed their Suburban into the side of his truck. The plan was to stun Ostopovich before two other officers challenged him to surrender, but Ostopovich didn't release his grip on the steering wheel after his vehicle was struck.

Out of the corner of his eye, Tim saw Jim getting out of the Suburban, but he decided there was no time to get out and run for cover behind the truck where the officers were to hide from potential gunfire. Ostopovich leveled a rifle at Tim, prompting the officer to crouch down under the console behind the engine block. Tim fired two shots from his police rifle through the Suburban's windshield, then he peered up, unsure whether he'd hit Ostopovich. Ostopovich's rifle, however, was still aimed at Tim, so the officer fired a third shot and then got out of the vehicle, hearing two rounds go past him.

When the gunfire came to an end, Jim had been shot in the back. He died near the gunman's home as colleagues desperately tried to keep him alive. After the fifty-five-year-old officer was hit, Ostopovich was shot by police. The gunman later died in hospital of blood loss from the twelve bullets that hit him in the head, neck, chest, arms, and left leg.

Months before Ostopovich died in the hail of bullets, he had threatened to kill Mounties at the local detachment. He'd been on and off his medication since being diagnosed in 2002 with a mental illness rendering him paranoid and delusional.

Jim Galloway had spent thirty-one years on the force and put his retirement on hold because of his love for the job. He was known as a legend in the RCMP police-dog service and had been a friend of Ron's for nineteen years. The loss for Ron was heartbreaking.

Ron's wife knew he was struggling with Jim's death and asked if he would get help after that emotional day in the kitchen. Three months later, he was approached by a former policing partner.

"She just looked at me and asked 'How you doing?' Then 'How you *really* doing?'" said Ron. "She said, 'You're not our Ronnie, you're too quiet.'"

At that time, Ron was working in the RCMP major crimes unit, investigating an average of twenty-three homicides a year and spending 120 days away from home. It was a stressful environment, which he blamed for his change in demeanour.

After responding to traumatic events and dealing with death for twenty-three years, deep down Ron knew something was terribly wrong. His mind was revisiting things that had occurred twenty years ago, and he couldn't make them disappear, but Ron was too scared to admit to anybody he might have a problem.

"I thought, 'Oh, crap, I'm busted. If she knows, everybody else knows, so what's going to happen?'" he said. "I thought I was going to lose my job. That's still the mentality. That's one of the big impediments to our people or any other police service—members stepping forward and saying I need help because they are so afraid of being stigmatized, ostracized, and isolated."

Three weeks later, Ron did one of the most frightening things of his career—he reached out for help. It took him three attempts to make the call. He'd never been so scared in his life and wondered if it was the beginning of the end.

Ron was eventually diagnosed with Post-Traumatic Stress Disorder (PTSD), along with a major depressive disorder. Three months into therapy, however, his therapist stepped away from practice and Ron then didn't see anybody for nine months. Meanwhile the work in the major crimes unit remained busy, and the death toll kept mounting.

Ron began experiencing feelings of inadequacy, guilt, embarrassment, and anger. Not knowing where those feelings were coming from, he distanced himself from personal relationships, especially with his wife.

"I didn't want to talk to anybody. My wife would have to literally make me phone my mother. I was trying to alienate my wife; I was trying to get her to leave me. I was trying to get her to a place where she would just hate me, so when I killed myself she wouldn't care," said Ron, adding he didn't want to unload on her since she had enough to worry about every time he walked out the door.

Working as a crisis negotiator, Ron admits there were times he would walk out from behind cover, hoping somebody would take a shot.

"I just didn't care. The pain is so intense; the helplessness is so intense that the only way for us to escape that is death."

The suicidal thoughts lasted for at least eighteen months. It was the lowest Ron had ever felt in his life. He wasn't just thinking about killing himself; he had a plan to make his death look like an accident by driving at a high speed into an abutment on the 17th Street overpass along Yellowhead Trail. One night when his wife was at work, Ron went to look at the location, but he drove home after an Edmonton Police officer stopped and asked what he was doing.

On another occasion, Ron was in his basement drinking heavily, with his loaded service weapon at his side. His dog had been asleep on the floor, but he suddenly came up to Ron and put his head on his lap, then sniffed the gun. Ron decided to unload the weapon and stuff it down the couch.

Realizing something wasn't right, Ron's family eventually held an intervention and guided him to a trauma specialist—a woman he says saved his life. Her questions were different. Her approach was different. Ron finally felt like he had met someone who understood what he was going through.

"I connected with her. It was the first time I had some optimism. Even through that darkness I could see light at the end of the tunnel," he said. "I learned to trust her very quickly and put so much faith in her that she was going to save me. I am so grateful for that woman and she knows it."

The fifty-six-year-old is now at peace with who he is—a feeling he never thought would come. Working in communications at RCMP K-Division in Edmonton, Ron attends conferences across North America, speaking about his experience with PTSD. His talks about the subject represent some of the most empowering work he's ever done. Looking back at the person he was five years ago leaves him flabbergasted, but depression is something Ron will never escape.

"I live with a disorder, but it will not ruin me, it will not control my life anymore," he said. "I will control it. I refuse to be a victim."

Ron is amazed his wife stuck by his side and is still with him to this day. He owes her everything after giving her every reason not to stick with him as he waded through his personal turmoil, doing everything he could to push her away. It was only in the last couple of years that Ron has been able to forgive himself for how badly he treated his lifelong partner. He never got physical with her, but he could use words like a sword, often leaving deep wounds.

One of the biggest challenges on his road to recovery was figuring out who he was without the badge. Ron now feels he can leave the RCMP with peace of mind, rather than feeling like he lost a part of himself.

"You hear so many of my generation say this isn't what we do, this is who we are. You can look at that either as an admirable statement or a very unhealthy statement, and I choose the latter. You normalize what you do. It becomes this over-identification with the badge, that person that you're trying to live up to," said Ron, who has no regrets about his thirty-four years of policing because to him the good far outweighs the bad.

"Police officers have a helper mentality and that's why they are drawn to public service," he said. "The problem is, to be a helper you got to have a heart. But when you have a heart, sometimes it gets broken. We don't like to admit that, because you're there to fix everyone else's problems and make sure they go home safe. You put yourself second."

SOURCES

MaryAnn Plett: Edmonton Police, *Edmonton Sun*,
reporter's notes, Unsolved Murders / Missing People
Canada (www.unsolvedcanada.ca).

Karen Ewanciw: Reporter's notes, Edmonton Police,
Edmonton Sun.

HUB Mall Triple Murder: Reporter's notes, *Edmonton
Sun*, CBC News.

Red Light Lounge Massacre: *Edmonton Sun*, *Edmonton
Journal*, Last Link on the Left (www.lastlinkontheleft.
com).

Melissa Jane Letain: *Edmonton Sun*, reporter's notes,
Unsolved Murders / Missing People Canada (www.
unsolvedcanada.ca).

Life in the Homicide Unit: Reporter's notes.

The "Punky" Case and DNA: Reporter's notes,
Edmonton Sun, *Edmonton Journal*.

Lillian Berube: *Edmonton Sun*, reporter's notes, Last
Link on the Left (www.lastlinkontheleft.com).

Charlotte Baas: *Edmonton Sun*, reporter's notes.

Marie Goudreau: *Edmonton Sun*, reporter's notes,
Unsolved Murders / Missing People Canada (www.
unsolvedcanada.ca).

Barb Danelesko: *Edmonton Sun*, *Edmonton Journal*.

Missing Persons and the Case of Lyle and Marie McCann: Reporter's notes, *Edmonton Sun*.

Robert Brodyk: Reporter's notes, *Edmonton Sun*.

Wayne Kreutz: *Edmonton Sun*, reporter's notes.

Sangeeta Khanna: *Edmonton Sun*, reporter's notes.

Johnny Altinger: *Edmonton Sun*, reporter's notes, court transcripts.

Victims of Homicide: Reporter's notes, *Edmonton Sun*, *Edmonton Journal*.

Sheila Salter: *Edmonton Sun*, *Edmonton Journal*, reporter's notes.

Cathy Greeve: *Edmonton Sun*, *Edmonton Journal*, reporter's notes.

Mir Hussain: *Edmonton Sun*.

Tania Murrell: *Edmonton Sun*, *Edmonton Journal*.

Project KARE: Reporter's notes, *Edmonton Sun*.

Lisa Kopf: Reporter's notes, *Edmonton Sun*.

The Gruesome: *Edmonton Sun*, reporter's notes, Last Link on the Left (www.lastlinkontheleft.com).

Gail McCarthy: *Edmonton Sun*, reporter's notes.

The Somalis: *Edmonton Sun*, *The Globe and Mail*, reporter's notes.

Wrong Place, Wrong Time: *Edmonton Sun*, *Edmonton Journal*.

Brenda McClenaghan: *Edmonton Sun*, *Edmonton Journal*.

Here Today, Gone Tomorrow: *Edmonton Sun*, reporter's notes.

Dylan McGillis: *Edmonton Sun*, reporter's notes.

Liana White: *Edmonton Sun*.

No Rhyme or Reason: *Edmonton Sun*, reporter's notes.

Shernell Pierre and Nadine Robinson-Creary: *Edmonton Sun*, reporter's notes.

The Mandins: *Edmonton Sun*, *Edmonton Journal*, Parole Board of Canada documents.

Izaac Middleton and James Milliken: *Edmonton Sun*, reporter's notes.

Constable Ezio Faraone: *Edmonton Sun*, *Edmonton Journal*, reporter's notes.

Police and PTSD: Reporter's notes, *Edmonton Sun*.

ABOUT THE AUTHOR

A journalist since 2003, Pamela Roth has spent the bulk of her career covering court and crime for various newspapers in Alberta, Canada. She began working on the crime desk at the *Edmonton Sun* in October 2010 and moved to Victoria, B.C., in 2015, to work as an editor with the *Victoria News*. An avid traveller, she also specializes in travel writing.